Family Health and Fitness

FROSTIES

Family Health and Fitness

Dr. Alan Maryon-Davis

Sundial

Contents

First published in 1981 by Octopus Books Limited
59 Grosvenor Street, London W1

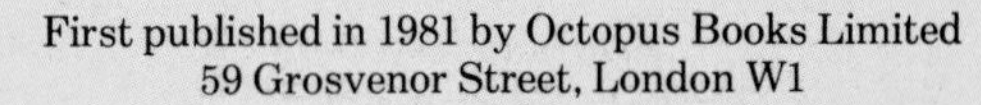

ISBN 0 906320 26 7

Printed in England by Severn Valley Press Limited

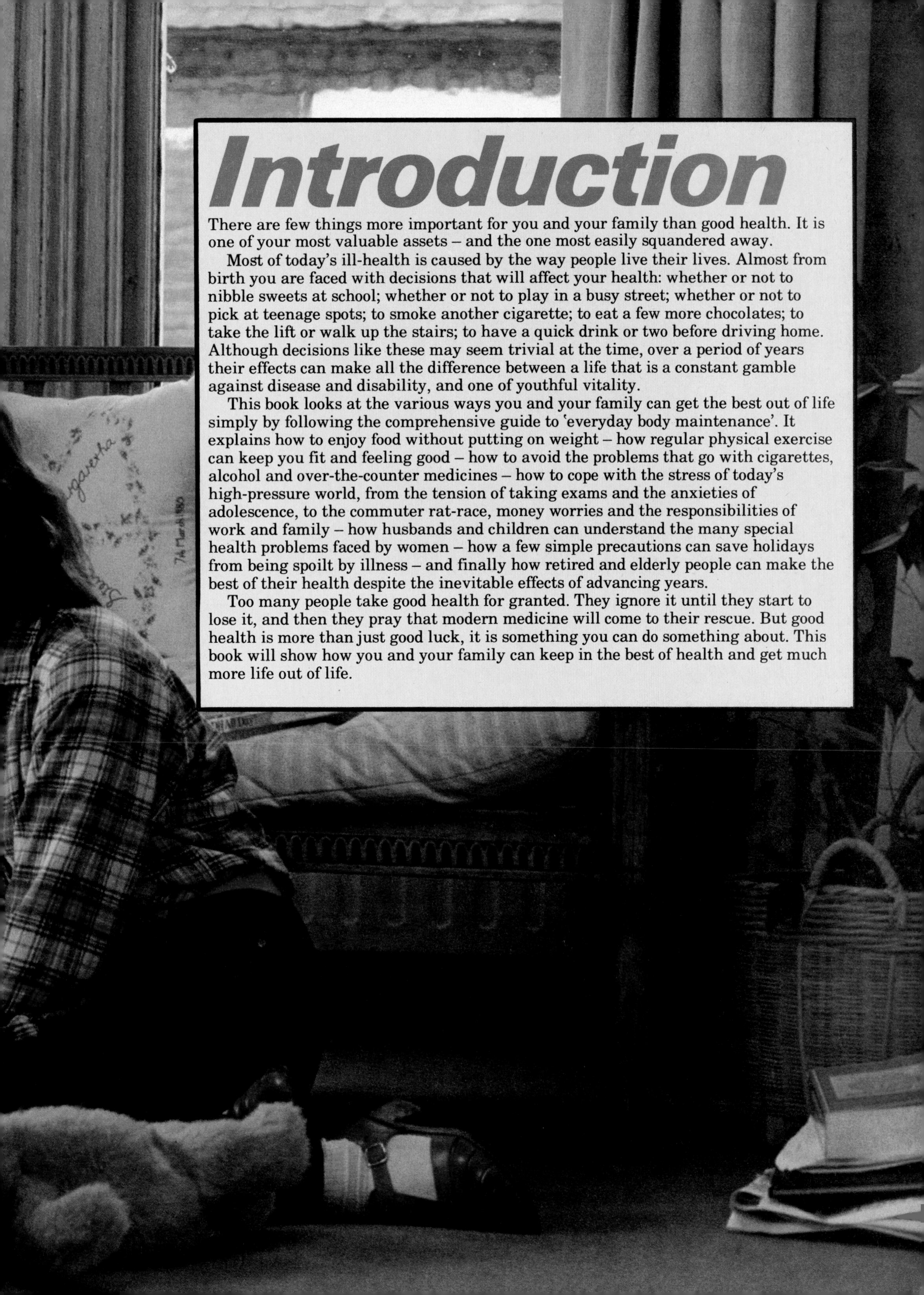

Introduction

There are few things more important for you and your family than good health. It is one of your most valuable assets – and the one most easily squandered away.

Most of today's ill-health is caused by the way people live their lives. Almost from birth you are faced with decisions that will affect your health: whether or not to nibble sweets at school; whether or not to play in a busy street; whether or not to pick at teenage spots; to smoke another cigarette; to eat a few more chocolates; to take the lift or walk up the stairs; to have a quick drink or two before driving home. Although decisions like these may seem trivial at the time, over a period of years their effects can make all the difference between a life that is a constant gamble against disease and disability, and one of youthful vitality.

This book looks at the various ways you and your family can get the best out of life simply by following the comprehensive guide to 'everyday body maintenance'. It explains how to enjoy food without putting on weight – how regular physical exercise can keep you fit and feeling good – how to avoid the problems that go with cigarettes, alcohol and over-the-counter medicines – how to cope with the stress of today's high-pressure world, from the tension of taking exams and the anxieties of adolescence, to the commuter rat-race, money worries and the responsibilities of work and family – how husbands and children can understand the many special health problems faced by women – how a few simple precautions can save holidays from being spoilt by illness – and finally how retired and elderly people can make the best of their health despite the inevitable effects of advancing years.

Too many people take good health for granted. They ignore it until they start to lose it, and then they pray that modern medicine will come to their rescue. But good health is more than just good luck, it is something you can do something about. This book will show how you and your family can keep in the best of health and get much more life out of life.

Bodycare

Skin

We are born with a beautifully soft, smooth and delicate skin and throughout childhood, despite the usual quota of cuts, grazes, bites, stings and plain old dirt, our skin fares surprisingly well. Young skin has remarkable powers of regeneration, and most of these insults are shrugged off with each new layer of fresh skin cells.

In puberty, however, the skin begins to change. Under the influence of sex hormones it becomes thicker and more hairy, much more so in boys than in girls, and the sebaceous glands start to secrete more sebum, the skin's natural oil. For most teenagers this heralds the embarrassing problem of acne.

From adulthood onwards the main influence on the health of our skin is time itself. Rather like carbon copies, the deeper layers of skin are constantly multiplying and replenishing those nearer the surface. As carbon paper deteriorates with repeated use, so much the same thing happens to skin with

Following a few basic guidelines on everyday skincare will keep your complexion as clear and healthy as a child's.

the passage of time. Although the cells are always being renewed these 'copies' have less and less of the clarity of the original. In other words the skin shows signs of age and the clear bloom of youth slowly but steadily gives way to the sags and wrinkles of later years.

In a largely vain attempt to delay this inevitable process, people spend a great deal of time, trouble and money on pampering their skin in order to resist wear and tear but not because they are concerned about maintaining its vital functions (regulating body temperature, conserving body fluid, repelling bacteria). Their major concern is to look good; because looking good goes a long way towards feeling good.

The condition of the skin is a reflection of both health and fortune. Apart from the scars of cuts, grazes and acne, damage can follow the use of detergents and solvents. Chronic illness and dietary deficiency also take their toll and over-exposure to sun and wind add to the ravages of time.

Nevertheless some of these threats can be averted, and by taking a little extra care and following a few basic guidelines you can do much to maintain the health and appearance of your skin.

Your Face

Everyday skincare is very much simpler than the cosmetics industry would have you believe. The most important principle is that your skin should be kept clean, without removing so much of its natural oil (sebum) that it becomes too dry. Your choice of cleanser will therefore depend on the oiliness of your skin. An oily skin should be cleansed with mild soap and water. To prevent roughening do not use water that is too hot and blot dry with a soft towel rather than rub. For a dry skin even mild soap may be too harsh, removing what little oil there is. Use a cleansing cream or lotion instead, which lifts off make-up, dirt, and skin-scales without degreasing it. Most people's faces have so-called 'combination skins', which means oily with dry patches. The dry areas can be protected by smoothing in a 'moisturizer' after cleansing with mild soap. A moisturizer is simply an emollient (softening) preparation which replaces the skin's natural oil and prevents excessive drying.

Treatment is sometimes advised to tighten sagging contours and freshen the skin. It consists of exercises and massage which impart a temporary soothing, refreshing feeling and a glowing flush. Unfortunately it does nothing to prevent sags or wrinkles.

Facial saunas have a similar temporary effect and are also useless in the long term.

Face-masks leave the skin feeling beautifully smooth and dry by absorbing oil and moisture but again the effect is only temporary.

Preparations which claim to 'feed' the skin with 'natural substances', such as collagen or avocado, or rejuvenate it by removing lines and wrinkles, are misleading since skin cannot be nourished in any way other than via the bloodstream and lines and wrinkles can only be removed by cosmetic surgery. However, such preparations are at worst harmless and at best comforting.

No-one's skin can escape the ravages of time and how quickly one's skin shows signs of age depends on many factors including heredity. Long-term exposure to strong sunlight certainly speeds up the process (see page 14), and contrary to popular belief, fresh air and exercise have no specifically beneficial effect on one's complexion.

Acne

Everyone at some time in his life has acne, the all-too-familiar spots and pustules that occur particularly on the face, but also may affect the neck, back and chest. It is at its worst in the self-conscious teen years.

Acne is caused by excessive secretions of sebum, not by having dirty skin. Usually the skin of acne-sufferers shows other signs of over-greasiness such as *blackheads* and *whiteheads*. Over-greasiness is usually the result of hormonal imbalance, which frequently accompanies normal adolescence. About two out of three women suffer from spots in the week before their period, again because of hormone changes.

Acne clears up eventually, but in severe cases can lead to permanent pock marking of the face. However, with simple treatment, it can be vastly improved within a few months and scarring avoided.

1. Most important: *never* pick or squeeze spots.
2. Avoid over-washing; twice a day is quite often enough. Use hot water and a medicated soap if you like. Towel dry briskly. If you use a face flannel make sure it's clean.
3. Get plenty of sunshine. Ultraviolet light is usually beneficial in moderation.
4. There is no evidence that fatty foods make acne worse, although acne sufferers are usually advised to avoid eating chocolate.
5. If you use make-up, avoid creams and oil-based cosmetics.
6. Medicated lotions (non-prescription) may be helpful, particularly those containing sulphur, resorcinol, salicylic acid or benzoyl peroxide.
7. If all these measures fail to control the acne within a few months, see your doctor.

Cleansing

This means removing make-up, dirt and skin-scales, and for those with oily skins it also means removing excess sebum.

Oily skin should be cleansed with a mild soap and warm water. If the water is too hot it can lead to peeling and also dilatation (widening) of skin blood vessels. Blot dry with a soft towel rather than rub.

For a dry skin even mild soap may be too harsh. Use a cleansing cream or lotion instead.

For 'combination skins' (oily with dry patches) cleanse with a mild soap and correct any dryness with a moisturizer.

Toning This means freshening and tightening the skin. Toners (or fresheners) are 'astringent', which means that they evaporate quickly, cooling the skin and making the tiny skin muscles contract. This gives a temporary feeling of freshness. Some contain alcohol which removes grease from the hair follicles ('pores').

Moisturizing This means adding an oil to the outer layers of the skin, which smooths and softens it and helps it to retain moisture. Moisturizing is only necessary if the skin's natural oil, sebum, has been removed by cleansing (e.g. after using soap) or if the skin is naturally too dry.

Hands

The skin on your hands has its own built-in protection to guard against daily wear and tear. The thick surface on the palm responds to physical and chemical irritation by growing still thicker, and pads of leathery skin, or calluses, develop to protect against pressure and abrasion. On the backs of the hands the skin is thin but quick to heal and nails protect the fingertips.

Hardworking hands soon look and feel rough, for frequent washing in soap and detergent removes the skin's natural moisturizing oil and leads to drying, cracking, and eventually, chapping. Frequent contact with chemicals, detergents, or allergens (from various plants, animals, and the nickel in inexpensive jewellery) can cause dermatitis or eczema.

When performing household tasks wear rubber gloves for protection, whenever possible, but remove them every two hours to allow perspiration to evaporate. Barrier creams are useful for repelling solvents and corrosives, and keeping grease and grime from the skin, while emollient creams help keep the skin soft and should be used after hands have been immersed in hot, soapy water.

Nails A complete fingernail takes from three to six months to grow, but its quality and shape are affected by a variety of factors. Vitamin and iron deficiency can cause thinning, softening and deformity, while damage to the base of the nail (such as that caused by a blow) may disrupt its formation and cause pitting or grooving. Nails can become brittle, so they crack and split if too frequently exposed to hot water, domestic cleansers or nail varnish remover.

There are no simple remedies for brittle nails but creams and oils can help to protect them against heat and chemicals while rubber gloves keep hot water away. Nail polish is protective, as well as attractive, but always use an oily remover.

Regular manicuring helps to prevent problems as well as to improve the nails' appearance. Cutting and smoothing the nail edge prevents snagging and tearing, and this should be done when they are softened after a warm bath. Use an emery board for filing nails and file towards the centre when they are dry and hardened.

Nail-biting is fairly harmless but can cause regression of the nailbed resulting in stubby nails. Nibbling or picking the skin at the sides of the nails may provide an entry for infection. To discourage the habit, try painting the nails with white iodine.

Feet

The skin on the feet is specially adapted to its weight-bearing task since the horny skin of the soles is designed to respond to pressure and abrasion by thickening up rapidly to form protective pads or calluses.

The soles of the feet, like the palms of the hands, have no hair or sebaceous glands, but have an abundance of sweat glands, which, in a natural state, would keep them moist and supple, and improve their grip. When enclosed in shoes, however, the dampness of the feet encourages the growth of skin fungi and bacteria and gives rise to several skin problems, including foot odour and athlete's foot (tender itchy peeling skin specially between the toes). Children's feet can get very hot and sweaty, particularly if they wear plastic, artificial leather or man-made fibre shoes or trainers which are often poorly ventilated. Shoes should be allowed to air at least every other day. Socks, stockings or tights should be changed every day.

Feet should be bathed daily in warm soapy water and dried briskly with a towel, especially over the sole and between the toes. Apply talc liberally (a fungicidal talc will help clear athlete's foot) and moisturizing creams and oils may help to temporarily soften calluses.

Nails Toenails grow at a quarter the rate of fingernails, so it takes about a year to grow a complete nail. A pedicure should follow the same principles as a manicure, but it is important to cut toenails square across and not too close to the nailbed, otherwise ingrowing toenails may result. This painful inflammation, caused by the side-edge of the nail (nearly always the big toe) being pushed into the neighbouring skin, may also be caused by ill-fitting shoes.

Personal Hygiene

Body odour is an aspect of natural human function that has kept the soap and perfume industry busy for about 3000 years. Custom and tradition to some extent dictate how much is acceptable in decent company, but most people seek to avoid it.

The characteristic smell of body odour is somewhat musty and sickly. It is caused by the action of normal skin bacteria on the secretions of apocrine glands found on the skin around the armpits and genitals. The milky fluid produced tends to form a sticky coating on the hair shafts, so shaving can help to reduce the odour. Ordinary sweat (eccrine) glands produce a simple salty solution, which is not a source of body odour except on the feet.

Regular bathing not only removes accumulated dirt and grime but also washes away the dead skin, secretions and bacteria that cause body odour. Too little washing and we look, feel and smell dirty. Too much washing and there is a danger that the natural water-proofing oil will be washed out of the skin resulting in excessive dryness, peeling and eczema. However, this can be corrected with bath oil or emollient body lotion. A full bath every day may not be necessary depending on your occupation and daily activities, but daily soap and water to underarms, crotch and feet will help avoid body and foot odour.

Deodorant sprays and roll-ons contain an antiseptic ingredient which helps to prevent the odour-producing action of skin bacteria but this protection wears off as the deodorant becomes diluted with sweat.

Anti-perspirant sprays and roll-ons contain ingredients which reduce sweating. Roll-ons are more effective than sprays and generally cause less skin irritation. Many products combine both deodorant and anti-perspirant actions.

Enjoying bathtime. A chance to be together and to teach good hygiene habits.

Sun

For many people there are few more pleasant sensations than lying in the sun.

In fact, as far as the health of skin is concerned, sunlight is more damaging than it is beneficial, though it is true that some skin problems are improved by ultraviolet rays – particularly acne and psoriasis (a chronic inflammatory condition) – and that sunlight stimulates skin to produce vitamin D, needed in abundance by children going through the rapid growth spurt of puberty.

Many people know only too well the acute discomfort of being sunburnt (see page 73) when the skin becomes reddened and tender, and in severe cases, peels and blisters. Not so many people realize that sunlight can cause long term damage, either in the form of premature ageing, due to atrophy of the supporting tissue which results in the skin wrinkling and sagging and becoming covered with age freckles, or the development of skin tumours (including skin cancer) which mainly affects fair-skinned people in the tropics.

Sunburn is caused by medium wavelength ultraviolet (UVB) rays irritating the living layers of the skin. The rays are strongest in bright hot sun, but they can pass through cloud and can also be reflected off water, sand, or snow.

The skin protects itself against ultraviolet rays by thickening and developing a tan. This is a proliferation of the natural pigment, melanin, which absorbs the rays. Very fair-skinned people are especially vulnerable.

Unless the skin is already *well pigmented*, time spent in the sun should be strictly rationed. A fair-skinned person in a sunny resort should expose the skin for no more than 15 to 20 minutes on the first day, increasing by a third as much on each subsequent day until a tan begins to develop. Most toddlers and small children have skin which is very sensitive to sunlight, so carefully restrict their exposure to the sun for the first few days.

Providing sufficient care is taken with sunbathing, suncreams and lotions are unnecessary and do not speed up the natural tanning process. Some contain oil of bergamot, an artificial tanning accelerator, which sensitizes the skin to sunlight, but there are doubts about its long term safety. Genuine sunscreens and sunblocks, however, do afford a certain degree of protection.

Emollients These include suncreams and oils that only offer protection by reducing the drying effects of sun and wind.

Most people consider a full, healthy head of hair to be an extremely attractive feature – our 'crowning glory'. The key to healthy hair is moderation: wash your hair regularly but not too frequently with mild shampoo, and dry and brush it gently. Damage to the hair may be caused by excessive heat or drying, and by chemicals such as bleaches, dyes and detergents.

Sunscreens These are lotions, creams or oils containing an ingredient which is opaque to the burning UVB rays and thus blocks them. They allow most of the longer wave, non-burning, tanning UVA rays to reach the skin.

Sunblocks These are lotions, creams or oils containing an ingredient which is opaque to both types of ultraviolet rays, reducing the risk of burning but also preventing tanning. They are ideal protection for very fair-skinned people and for children.

Sun Lamps These offer an all-year-round tan. Inevitably, though, they have their drawbacks. Firstly, a conventional ultraviolet lamp produces predominantly UVB rays which tend to cause reddening and sunburn and more importantly, can cause eye damage. Sun lamps must be used carefully in accordance with the manufacturer's instructions. A more recent type of ultraviolet lamp, fluorescent tubes often in a 'sunbed', emit UVA rays which give a 'safe' tan – but there are grave doubts about the long term effects.

Treatment for Sunburn The discomfort of sunburn can be relieved by cooling the skin. Protect it from the sun by moving into the shade or covering the affected part with clothing. A bath in cool water or a sponge down with cold water will be very soothing.

If the discomfort is severe, two soluble aspirin or paracetamol tablets will give temporary relief. Calamine Lotion applied to the skin will cool it for a while. If blisters occur, do not prick them; it can lead to infection.

Hair

Hair, unlike skin, is dead. A healthy head of hair usually refers to a full growth of soft, shining hair. The skin's natural softener, sebum, is produced by the sebaceous gland in each hair follicle and is retained by the hair until it is washed out with soap or detergent. Sebum makes hair soft and shining, but it also attracts dirt and grime, especially in the polluted atmosphere of towns and cities.

Washing Hair should be shampooed no more often than is necessary to keep it clean, or, if the scalp is itchy, to keep it comfortable. Once or twice a week is usually sufficient. Too frequent washing may cause damage by removing the sebum and the scalp may react by eventually becoming much greasier. Always use a mild shampoo since this is less likely to cause brittle hair.

Conditioners These contain ingredients such as glycerine and waxes, which temporarily coat the hair to give a smooth, shiny surface.

Drying Wet hair is soft, stretchy and easy to scuff or split. It should be dabbed dry and combed or brushed very gently. Hold electric dryers well away from the hair.

Brushing and Combing Gentle brushing not only helps to keep hair tangle free, it also removes some of the grime, and spreads the sebum along the hairshaft making it soft and shining. However, over-vigorous brushing can break hairs off at the roots.

Dandruff Everyone has dandruff (flecks of dead scalp matted together with sebum) to some degree, since it is a normal consequence of the natural replacement of scalp cells. The best treatment is regular washing with a mild shampoo and gentle brushing. Some medicated shampoos, containing selenium or zinc pyrithione do seem to help.

Headlice This is the commonest hair problem amongst children, often transmitted from borrowed combs and brushes. Headlice are soft white wingless insects who live by sucking blood from the scalp. They cling to the hair roots and lay their eggs (called 'nits') on the hairshafts. Lice are equally at home in long or short hair, clean or dirty.

Any child with an itchy head should be inspected in a good light for nits and if any are found the *whole family* should be treated with a lice-eradicating lotion obtainable from the chemists. Ordinary shampoos will not help at all.

Eyes

Because they are so vulnerable the eyes are remarkably well-protected. They are shielded from direct blows by the bony prominences of forehead and cheeks; eyebrows and eyelashes help to keep out grit and grime; and blinking sweeps tear fluid over the eyeball's covering membrane (the conjunctiva) constantly keeping it moist, dust free and clear of infection. The eye is further protected from bright light by an automatic contraction of the iris (the coloured part of the eye), by partial closing of the eyelids and by lowering the eyebrows.

Routine cleansing consists of nothing more than a gentle wipe across the closed eyes with a clean tissue or face flannel moistened with warm water, with or without soap, to remove any dried secretions that have accumulated during sleep. Make-up can be removed in the same way or, if water-resistant, by using special remover. If eye make-up is left on overnight, it can clog the delicate glands on the eyelids.

Eyestrain

The eyes themselves cannot be 'strained' by too much close work in poor light, but the surrounding facial muscles may ache through overwork – usually in attempting to sharpen a dim image. The same muscles may ache in conditions of very bright light.

To avoid eyestrain, do not spend too long working in a poor light, or if necessary, rest your facial muscles by closing your eyes for a minute or two every half-an-hour.

Bright sunlight, especially if reflected off the sea, sand, or snow, can cause eyestrain by fatiguing the facial muscles. Sunglasses, especially those with polarized lenses, can help to avoid this by cutting down glare.

Ears

Ears have their own cleaning system. Soft wax is secreted by special glands in the ear canal and very slowly works its way out, carrying dirt and grime with it. The wax also has antiseptic properties. It should be removed from the outer ear with a finger or towel, and the outer ear cleaned with soap and water. Do not attempt to clean the inside of the ear canal.

Sometimes earwax hardens and blocks the ear canal, causing muffled hearing and discomfort. If this happens, a few drops of warm olive oil or glycerine helps to soften the wax sufficiently to remove it with a twist of cotton wool. If it persists try an earwax solvent from the chemist or see your doctor.

Prolonged exposure to very loud sounds can cause permanent, partial hearing loss. This is an occupational disease for those who work in extremely noisy surroundings, but it can also affect young people constantly exposed to very loud music.

Mouth, Teeth and Gums

Dental diseases are among the most widespread and most easily preventable of all maladies. In the UK, the figures are particularly worrying – about one in every ten five-year-olds has rampant tooth decay, and four out of every ten will need some sort of denture before the age of twenty-one. One adult in three has no natural teeth at all.

Many people seem to accept tooth decay and dentures as an inescapable fact of life. Yet with a little daily care and attention the full complement of healthy teeth can be kept well into old age. Regular dental check-ups are most important from early childhood onwards.

Everyone has two sets of natural teeth; the initial set of baby teeth or 'milk' teeth are gradually replaced by a set of permanent teeth that appear from the age of six or seven.

Teeth begin as minute buds deep within the jaws and begin to erupt about six months after birth until the set is complete at about the age of two. At about six years old, the process of replacement begins, finishing around the age of twelve or thirteen. The four rear molars (wisdom teeth) may not erupt until the late teens or early twenties, if at all.

Although the baby teeth are replaced as part of natural development, it is important to avoid losing them too soon through tooth decay. They act as a guide for the erupting permanent teeth.

Tooth Decay

Tooth decay, or dental caries, is a progressive destruction of the tooth crown. This is caused by acid eating away the tooth enamel and dentine to form a cavity which slowly, but steadily, increases in size. At first this causes tenderness, then agony and finally the loss of the tooth. The acid is produced by the action of bacteria on sugar residues left in the mouth after eating, especially the light concentrated sugar contained in sweets, soft drinks, preserves, cakes and biscuits. The bacteria are held in a soft sticky substance called 'plaque' which begins to form quite soon after sugary food has been in the mouth, appearing first in the cracks and crevices around the gum margins and between the teeth, and eventually covering the whole tooth surface making it look dull and yellow, and feel rough to the tongue.

The most striking way of showing the plaque on your teeth is to suck a plaque-disclosing tablet obtainable from the chemist's. This contains a vegetable dye which stains the plaque bright red but leaves the clean tooth surfaces uncoloured.

Children are particularly susceptible to tooth decay, partly because they tend to eat more sweets and sugary things than adults, and also because their tooth enamel seems to be less resistant.

Fluoride is a mineral present in natural drinking water in several parts of the country. At a dilution of one part per million it has been shown to protect against tooth decay. If present in the body while the teeth are actually developing, fluoride becomes incorporated into the enamel making it more acid-resistant and is therefore especially effective for infants and children.

Drinking water in most parts of the UK contains insufficient natural fluoride to prevent tooth decay, but studies have shown that in areas where the water is either naturally or artificially fluoridated tooth decay amongst children has been approximately halved.

Some people object to fluoridation on the principle that it is adding an artificial chemical to drinking water and is therefore a form of 'mass medication' over which the individual has no control. Health and medical authorities, however, have reported firmly in favour of fluoridation and repudiated any suggestion that it may be harmful to health.

Fluoride can also be obtained through tablets and drops but especially through fluoride toothpaste. Most of the research studies support the idea that fluoride toothpaste can help to prevent tooth decay if left in contact with the teeth for several minutes before rinsing it out.

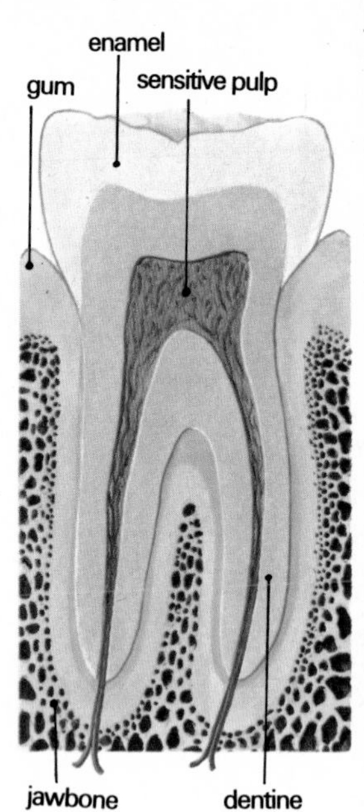

An adult normally has 32 permanent teeth, 16 to each jaw. On each side of either the upper or lower jaw (counting from the front backwards) are:
2 incisors (cutters)
1 canine (tearer)
2 premolars (shearers)
3 molars (grinders)
Despite differences in shape, all these teeth have the same basic structure (see diagram). Each tooth consists mostly of a thick shell of dentine (a hard calcareous tissue) surrounding a very sensitive pulp which contains a nerve and blood vessels. The exposed 'crown' of the tooth is covered by a protective layer of enamel which is very hard. The root (or roots in the case of the molars) sits in a gum-lined socket in the jawbone and is held in place by tough fibrous anchoring strands and a cement-like substance. The jaw is covered with soft gum tissue which surrounds the tooth forming a tight pocket about the enamel line.

A varied diet (see page 22) provides more than enough calcium and Vitamin D for healthy teeth. Without question the most important dietary danger to teeth is eating or drinking sugary things particularly between meals. The more often you have sugar in your mouth the more your teeth are attacked by acid. If you must nibble or sip something, nuts, crisps, cheese, raw fruit or vegetables and low-calorie drinks are much safer for your teeth.

Periodontal (Gum) Disease

Almost everybody who has any natural teeth has some degree of gum disease, if only a little tenderness and slight bleeding after brushing. For those over the age of 35, it is the most common dental disease. At its worst, healthy teeth are lost because the disease process affects the sockets, destroying the anchoring fibres and weakening the cementum. The tooth either works loose and falls out or is killed at the root and has to be extracted. As with dental caries, the enemy is plaque, but with gum disease it is inflammation caused by the bacteria themselves. Plaque forms at the neck of the tooth and between the teeth where it is likely to be missed by hurried brushing. The irritated gums become swollen and tender, so that they bleed easily. They may become infected, forming pus and causing foul breath, until eventually, the bony sockets themselves are destroyed and the teeth are lost.

How To Brush Your Teeth

Ideas about correct tooth brushing have changed since more has been discovered about plaque, gums and periodontal disease. It used to be considered incorrect to scrub back and forth along the teeth and correct to roll the brush vertically from the gums towards the crowns. Now it is known to be more important to get the bristles right into the nooks and crannies between gums and teeth to dislodge the plaque.

1. Choose a suitable toothbrush. Most dentists recommend a small-headed (never more than 25 mm (1 in), and even smaller for children) brush with nylon bristles that are not too hard.
Replace the brush when the bristles start to splay.
2. Use fluoride toothpaste.
3. It does not matter which teeth are brushed first, but always follow the same routine. Every surface of every tooth must be brushed, including the insides. Hold the brush so that it sits on the outer sides of two or three teeth at an angle of 45 degrees, the tips of the bristles slanting towards the gum (see diagram). Scrub back and forth firmly over these few teeth in very small, shuddering strokes. The bristle tips should slip into the gum pocket and dislodge any plaque. Spend several seconds at this before moving on to the next two or three teeth.
4. Having worked over the outer surfaces of all the teeth, do the same to the inner surfaces. These are more difficult to reach but it is vitally important not to neglect them. To reach behind the front teeth hold the brush vertically. Finish by brushing along all the biting surfaces.

Most people do not spend enough time cleaning their teeth really thoroughly to remove all the plaque. Always brush as well as you can, at least once a day. Careful brushing should reach most of the spaces between the teeth, although there are other techniques which may be helpful.

Dental floss is a strong waxed thread which, when stretched between the fingers, can be used to clean those areas missed by the toothbrush. Toothpicking is another way of dislodging plaque between the teeth.

Three minutes of careful brushing at least once a day is the most effective defence against tooth decay and gum disease.

Neck and Back

The human spine is a remarkable piece of engineering in the way it combines supporting strength with lithe mobility. It is able to withstand considerable stretching and compressing forces. It can be held firm and rigid or it can be bent and twisted in virtually any direction.

There are limits, however, to what the spine can achieve without strain and the possible causes of neck and back pain are many, ranging from poor posture, careless movement and lack of exercise to congenital malformation of the spine at birth or gradual (and sometimes sudden) degeneration in old age. However, the vast majority of neck and back pain sufferers are victims of a few common conditions.

Sharing the load – by carrying your shopping in each hand you will avoid unnecessary strain on your neck and back.

Sudden spinal pain

This includes such conditions as acute lumbago (backache in the small of the back), a stretched ligament (strain), a torn ligament (sprain), a dislocated vertebral joint or a 'slipped' intervertebral disc. These conditions come from either a sudden or prolonged stretching, bending or twisting of the spine and the resulting pain may be anything from a dull ache to a severe shooting pain.

It is quite common for spinal pain to be felt in parts of the body other than the spine. For example pain caused by neck injury might be felt in the shoulder or arm, and sciatica (an ache or shooting pain felt in the buttock and leg) often accompanies a slipped lumbar disc.

Long term spinal pain

This may be caused by one of three common problems: a previous back or neck injury which, although fully resolved at the time, leads to chronic intermittent trouble at a later stage; spinal deformity, which nearly everybody has to some extent either from birth, or from poor posture in the adolescent years; and spinal degeneration either of the discs (spondylosis) or of the tiny linking joints (osteoarthrosis) or of the vertebrae themselves (osteoporosis), all of which are natural consequences of getting older.

Back trouble in pregnancy

Backache is a common problem in the second half of pregnancy, caused initially by leaning back to balance the extra weight, and then, as childbirth approaches, by a hormonal loosening of the pelvic joints making them increasingly susceptible to strain.

How to avoid or minimize back trouble

Sudden neck and back trouble can be avoided, and years of suffering minimized by a few simple commonsense precautions.

1. Watch your posture Good deportment is vital and can help the whole family to avoid future back trouble. Sloppy posture can lead to the stretching of ligaments and muscles and the realignment of bones so that you become literally 'set' in whatever poor posture you usually adopt. This is especially true of teenagers whose bones are still developing.

When standing, the best advice is to 'stand tall', which means gently pulling in the tummy and easing the top of the pelvis backwards, so straightening the hollow of the back. It also means holding the shoulders gently back, the neck erect and keeping the chin tucked in. You do not have to be stiff and rigid to achieve this posture.

Jobs like washing-up or ironing should be done at working surfaces that are the correct height to avoid stooping.

For those who spend much of their lives sitting down, the two biggest sins are slouching and neck-drooping.

The lumbar spine should always be firmly supported and held straight when sitting, whether on a hard or soft seat. Long car journeys are a common cause of back trouble. Sit with your buttocks as far back into the seat as possible.

The correct height for a hard chair allows the feet to rest flat on the floor with the knees bent at 90 degrees. A desktop should be roughly level with the elbows when sitting correctly.

You spend a large proportion of your life in bed; to avoid postural problems, choose a firm mattress and, even more important, a firm base below the mattress. Pillows should support your neck in a horizontal straight line when you lie on your side.

2. Avoid Injury Necks and backs are easily injured by careless or violent action. Here are some ways to avoid such occurrences.

Bending This puts a great strain on the back. Keep it as straight and upright as possible, making the hips, knees and ankles do the bending.

Twisting Twisting suddenly, particularly to reach something behind you and especially when sitting down is a classic way to pull or wrick your back. Move gently – or better still, get a swivel chair.

Lifting and Carrying Careless lifting causes more back injury than any other activity. The golden rule is to keep the back straight and upright and the load as close to the body as possible. To pick up a heavy object (or child) crouch down instead of bending, put your arms right around it and pull it close to you before straightening your legs.

When carrying heavy shopping, have two baskets equally loaded, one in each hand. Better still, get a wheeled basket, but take care when carrying it up and down steps.

Blows and Falls Any severe or awkward blow or fall which jars the neck or back can do immediate damage and may cause chronic discomfort. This is a constant risk for anyone indulging in active sports, but can easily happen by falling at home or at work – down the stairs or off a chair or ladder.

3. Lose Weight It is obvious that the heavier you are the more stress and strain there is on your back when you stand, walk or bend. An effective reducing diet (see page 28) may be your best protection against back injury.

4. Exercise A few minutes each day spent mobilizing the spine and strengthening the trunk can greatly help to protect the neck and back from strains and sprains. A series of mobilizing exercises is shown on page 55.

Below are two trunk strengthening exercises. A tight tummy is particularly important because it acts like a firm splint and supports the back during exertion.

Back Strengthener Lie face downwards, arms by your sides, legs together. Raise your head and shoulders off the floor and look straight ahead. At the same time raise legs off the floor to about mid-thigh. Hold for about ten seconds then relax. Repeat this six times at the first attempt, but gradually build up to 20 repeats at each session.

Abdomen Strengthener Lie on your back, arms by your sides, legs together. Raise your legs and slowly perform large cycling movements with your legs, keeping your back flat on the floor and just grazing the floor with each heel as it circles round. Do ten slow 'pedals' – about 20 seconds activity – and then relax. Repeat this three times at your first attempt and gradually build up to ten at each session.

Firm, strong trunk muscles will help to protect your spine from strain or injury.

Back strengthener exercises

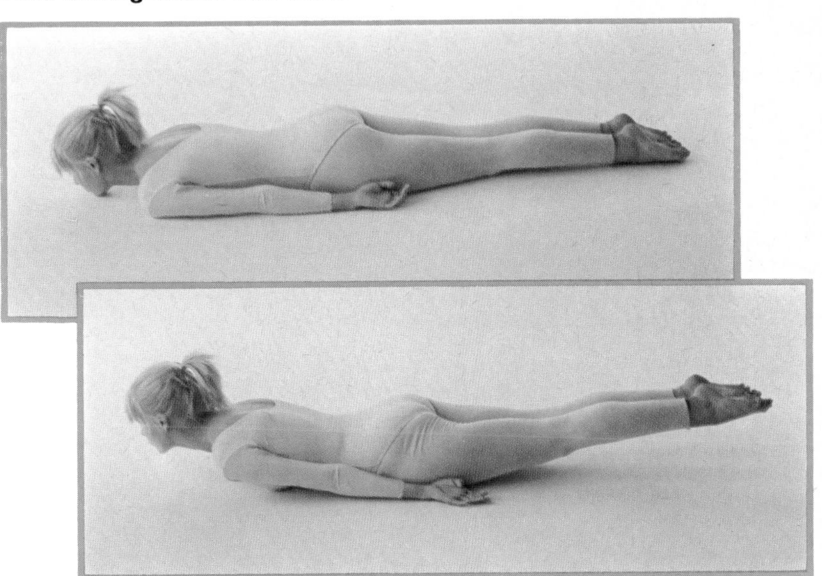

Abdomen strengthener exercises

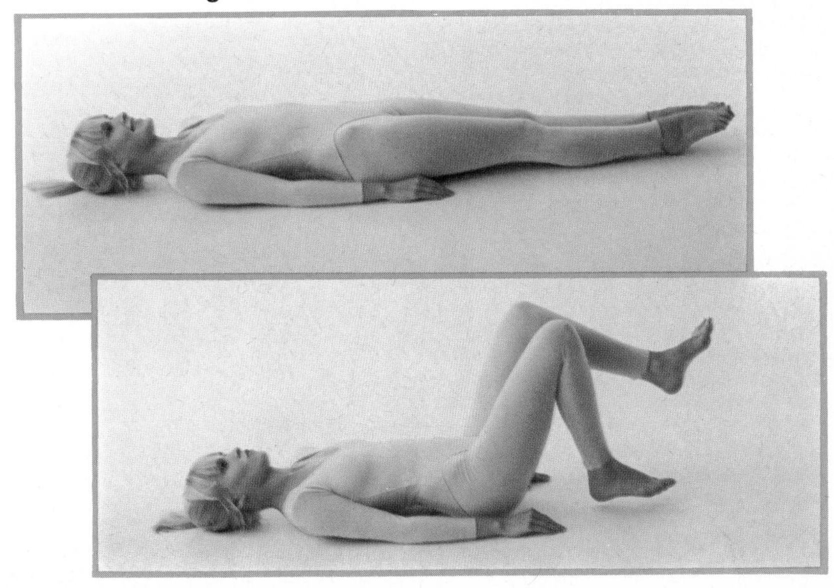

Guide to Good Eating

Striking a Balance

Eating sensibly is not so much a question of which are 'good' foods and which are 'bad' foods, as simply striking a balance between all the different sorts of food so that you get enough of each of them without eating too much of any. The golden rule is variety.

A balanced diet is one which provides just the right quantity, and no more, of each of the three fundamental dietary needs – nutrients, energy and fibre.

Nutrients

These are needed to provide the raw materials for growth, body functions, maintenance and tissue repair. Nutrients are obtained by digesting, absorbing and metabolizing the main food components:

Proteins provide essential amino acids needed for the body to make its own proteins which it uses for tissue growth, maintenance and repair, and enzyme and hormone production. It is a common misconception that the more protein-containing foods one eats, the more strong and vigorous one will be. In fact, the body needs only enough protein for normal growth and repair. Any extra will not stimulate extra growth; instead it is broken down and either excreted or stored as body fat. On average we eat about twice as much protein as we need.

Fats are turned into fatty acids and other fatty metabolites, most of which are used for energy production and stored as body fat. Most of us eat far more fat than we need.

Carbohydrates are sugars and starches which, like fats, are broken down to be used mainly for energy production and stored as body fat. On average we eat nearly three-quarters of our own weight in sugar *every year* – again much more than is beneficial.

Vitamins are needed in tiny quantities to catalyze and trigger many vital body processes. A good balanced diet provides all the vitamins necessary, and no amount of extra vitamins will make a healthy person any healthier. Indeed doctors are becoming increasingly worried about the possible dangers of vitamin overdose. Added vitamins are obviously important in those rare cases where people are genuinely undernourished or are eating a poorly balanced diet, which often applies to the elderly, to people living alone, to alcoholics or those that are chronically ill. For most people, however, extra vitamins are a waste of time and money.

Minerals are required for a large variety of purposes throughout the body, and include calcium for bones and teeth, and iron for blood. Again, a normal varied diet contains more than enough minerals.

Energy

This is needed to power the body machine; not only for movement and action, but also for the millions of energy consuming processes involved in the basic body chemistry, such as growth, functioning and repair of every tissue and organ in the body. It is provided by the chemical breakdown of the 'fuel' components of food; especially fats and carbohydrates. Energy is measured in calories (though nowadays scientists use kilojoules – 100 kJ equals 24 Cal).

Most people in this country eat far more energy-providing foods than they need, the result being that nearly half the nation is overweight.

Foods which claim to be 'packed with energy to give you extra vitality' are usually merely loaded with calories. They will not give you vitality, unless you happen to be literally starving. Indeed, if you have a tendency to put on weight, too much energy-rich food will make you fatter and if anything rather less energetic.

Fibre

This is needed to act as a 'conveyor belt' for the food components as they pass through the digestive system. It consists of undigested, unabsorbed gels, gums and fibres – the residue of plant material in the diet. Fibre used to be called roughage, but doctors have come to realize that it has important functions other than its gentle laxative action. It not only smoothes the passage of the intestinal contents, but it also controls the absorption of certain nutrients and energy-providing substances into the bloodstream.

Most people **do not eat enough** dietary fibre.

Making the choice

Remember that the way to choose wisely is to choose widely. To ensure a good supply of all the essential nutrients, the family shopping basket should have as varied a content as possible.

Nutritional problems usually only affect those people who tend to eat the same rather limited menu day after day. The most likely candidates for under-nutrition in this country are fanatical slimmers, food faddists, bereaved widowers living alone and babies weaned on strict vegetarian diets. In all these examples the missing ingredient is variety, an essential for a well-balanced diet.

Scales of justice? Obesity is the commonest result of an unbalanced diet.

Obesity

The commonest nutritional problem in most western societies is obesity.

The commonest cause of obesity (usually defined as being 20 per cent or more overweight), is the over-eating of energy-rich foods, particularly fat and sugar. Virtually all foods 'contain' calories (that is, energy is released when the foods are broken down in the body). Problems arise when more calories, and therefore more energy, are released than the body actually needs. Any energy that is not burnt up by physical exertion or the basic body chemistry is stored in the body, mostly as body fat (adipose tissue).

Why is it, though, that some people put on weight more easily than others, even if they eat the same amount? The answer is in the way their bodies cope with calories. Apart from fuelling body processes and physical exertion, energy is also used to produce and dissipate heat (a process known as thermogenesis). Recent research suggests that thin people who stay thin despite eating more than enough calories have a more efficient mechanism for thermogenesis and can therefore lose excess energy as heat. People with less efficient thermogenesis store the excess and so get fat.

Age and sex are two other factors involved. It is normal and natural for women to have more of their body weight in the form of fat. A healthy 20-year-old woman is 20–25 per cent fat, whereas her male counterpart is only 10–20 per cent. This difference becomes exaggerated as time goes on; a healthy 50-year-old woman may be 30–45 per cent fat, compared with only 20–25 per cent fat in a healthy 50-year-old man.

Whilst it does not always follow that fat children will become fat adults, it is certainly true that bad dietary habits learned in childhood are notoriously difficult to change. It is literally vital that children should be taught about healthy eating from infancy by their parents setting a good example.

There are also sex differences in the distribution of body fat. Men tend to put on weight around the trunk and on the face. Women tend to put it on the thighs, the breasts and the buttocks. The pattern is determined by your genes and you cannot alter it. Those places where you put weight on first are always the last to lose it when you slim. Claims that any particular exercise, diet, massage, vibrator, or any other 'spot reducer' can help you lose weight specifically from any particular part are simply not true. Nor is there any scientific evidence for the 'cellulite theory' – that is that the fat which dimples a woman's thighs is different from ordinary fat and will respond to specific treatments other than a standard reducing diet and exercise.

Staying slim seems to be one of the major obsessions of modern man – and even more so of modern woman. But apart from the cultural pressure to look lithe and lissome, how important is slimness to health?

The brief answer is that, statistically speaking, the more overweight you are, the younger you are likely to die. Added to that is the prospect that obesity increases the risk of suffering any of a long list of difficulties, disadvantages and diseases. These range from ordinary everyday things like having difficulty finding clothes that fit and general embarrassment, to more serious problems such as depression, marital disharmony, backache, foot trouble, arthritis, varicose veins, gallstones, shortness of breath, high blood pressure, diabetes, heart attack and stroke. Stay slim and you will have a better chance of avoiding these problems.

On the other hand, good health also means being happy and contented. There is no point in making life really miserable by trying to slim down to an unrealistic weight. As ever, it is a matter of striking the right balance . . . for you.

How fat are you?

Obviously if you look fat you almost certainly are fat. Try bobbing up and down naked in front of a full-length mirror – any rolls and pads of excess fat will be immediately apparent. Pinch the skin and subcutaneous fat at the back of your upper arm, midway between shoulder and elbow. If the skinfold is more than 2·5 cm (1 in) thick, you are likely to be obese and should consider dieting.

However, it really depends on the average thickness of fat spread all over your body frame. The taller and broader you are, the more you can weigh without having excess fat. The best way, therefore, to see if you are overweight is to check against the standard tables of desirable weights for your height and frame size. (Frame size corresponds approximately to chest measurement for men and hips for women.)

How to weigh yourself

If you have a tendency to put on weight easily you should weigh yourself regularly – but no more often than once a week.

1. Use the same scales each time and keep a note of your weight.
2. Wear the same amount of clothing – or none at all.
3. Weigh at the same time of day – body weight has a 24-hour cycle.

The tables opposite give the range of weight which is desirable for good health depending on height and 'frame size'.
You must judge your frame size for yourself, but you can get some idea from the width of your hip-bones if you are a woman, or the width of your rib-cage if you are a man.
These figures do not apply to growing children.

Desirable weights (in indoor clothing) for adults aged 25 and over

Men

Height (in shoes)			Weight					
			Small frame		Medium frame		Large frame	
m	ft	in	kg kg	st lb st lb	kg kg	st lb st lb	kg kg	st lb st lb
1·575	5	2	50·8–54·4	8 0– 8 8	53·5–58·5	8 6– 9 3	57·2–64·0	9 0–10 1
1·6	5	3	52·2–55·8	8 3– 8 11	54·9–60·3	8 9– 9 7	58·5–65·3	9 3–10 4
1·626	5	4	53·5–57·2	8 6– 9 0	56·2–64·7	8 12– 9 10	59·9–67·1	9 6–10 8
1·651	5	5	54·9–58·5	8 9– 9 3	57·6–63·0	9 1– 9 13	61·2–68·9	9 9–10 12
1·676	5	6	56·2–60·3	8 12– 9 7	59·0–64·9	9 4–10 3	62·6–70·8	9 12–11 2
1·702	5	7	58·1–62·1	9 2– 9 11	60·8–66·7	9 8–10 7	64·4–73·0	10 2–11 7
1·727	5	8	59·9–64·0	9 6–10 1	62·6–68·9	9 12–10 12	66·7–75·3	10 7–11 12
1·753	5	9	61·7–65·8	9 10–10 5	64·4–70·8	10 2–11 2	68·5–77·1	10 11–12 2
1·778	5	10	63·5–68·0	10 0–10 10	66·2–72·6	10 6–11 6	70·3–78·9	11 1–12 6
1·803	5	11	65·3–69·9	10 4–11 0	68·0–74·8	10 10–11 11	72·1–81·2	11 5–12 11
1·829	6	0	67·1–71·7	10 8–11 4	69·9–77·1	11 0–12 2	74·4–83·5	11 10–13 2
1·854	6	1	68·9–73·5	10 12–11 8	71·7–79·4	11 4–12 7	76·2–85·7	12 0–13 7
1·88	6	2	70·8–75·7	11 0–11 13	73·5–81·6	11 8–12 12	78·5–88·0	12 5–13 12
1·905	6	3	72·6–77·6	11 4–12 3	75·7–83·5	11 13–13 3	80·7–90·3	12 10–14 3
1·93	6	4	74·4–79·4	11 8–12 7	78·1–86·2	12 4–13 8	82·7–92·5	13 0–14 8

Women

Height (in shoes)			Weight					
			Small frame		Medium frame		Large frame	
m	ft	in	kg kg	st lb st lb	kg kg	st lb st lb	kg kg	st lb st lb
1·473	4	10	41·7–44·5	6 8– 7 0	43·5–48·5	6 12– 7 9	47·2–54·0	7 6– 8 7
1·499	4	11	42·6–45·8	6 10– 7 3	44·5–49·9	7 0– 7 12	48·1–55·3	7 8– 8 10
1·524	5	0	43·5–47·2	6 12– 7 6	45·8–51·3	7 3– 8 1	49·4–56·7	7 11– 8 13
1·549	5	1	44·9–48·5	7 1– 7 9	47·2–52·6	7 6– 8 4	50·8–58·1	8 0– 9 2
1·575	5	2	46·3–49·9	7 4– 7 12	48·5–54·0	7 9– 8 7	52·2–59·4	8 3– 9 5
1·6	5	3	47·6–51·3	7 7– 8 1	49·9–55·3	7 12– 8 10	53·5–60·8	8 6– 9 8
1·626	5	4	49·0–52·6	7 10– 8 4	51·3–57·2	8 1– 9 0	54·9–62·6	8 10– 9 12
1·651	5	5	50·3–54·0	7 13– 8 7	52·7–59·0	8 4– 9 4	56·8–64·4	8 13–10 2
1·676	5	6	51·7–55·8	8 2– 8 11	54·4–61·2	8 8– 9 9	58·5–66·2	9 3–10 6
1·702	5	7	53·5–57·6	8 6– 9 1	56·2–63·0	8 12– 9 13	60·3–68·0	9 7–10 10
1·727	5	8	55·3–59·4	8 10– 9 5	58·1–64·9	9 2–10 3	62·1–69·9	9 11–11 0
1·753	5	9	57·2–61·2	9 0– 9 9	59·9–66·7	9 6–10 7	64·0–71·7	10 1–11 4
1·778	5	10	59·0–63·5	9 4–10 0	61·7–68·5	9 10–10 11	65·8–73·9	10 5–11 9
1·803	5	11	60·8–65·3	9 8–10 4	63·5–70·3	10 0–11 1	67·6–76·2	10 9–12 0
1·829	6	0	62·6–67·1	9 12–10 8	65·3–72·1	10 4–11 5	69·4–78·5	10 13–12 5

The Fibre Factor

The average modern western diet contains relatively little fibre, the emphasis being on meat and dairy products, which contain no fibre at all. In addition, much of the plant food that we eat has had most of its fibre refined out – white flour, refined cereals and sugar are examples.

Medical evidence suggests that a low-fibre intake is linked not only with constipation but also with various bowel disorders including haemorrhoids (piles), diverticular disease and even perhaps cancer of the colon. Some experts believe that this low-fibre diet may also be partly responsible for the high incidence of obesity, diabetes and heart disease in developed countries.

An important point about unrefined high-fibre foods – such as wheatbran, wholemeal bread, wholewheat cereals, potatoes, peas, beans and lentils – is that they are satisfyingly filling without being packed with concentrated calories. Therefore, they provide the bulk of a meal without putting on extra weight – something which may come as a surprise to those slimmers who are convinced that bread and potatoes are evil.

Which foods have most fibre?
All unrefined plant foods contain fibre, but some in greater quantity than others.

The easiest way to increase the fibre in the family's diet is to replace white bread with wholemeal. Weight-for-weight, the latter has four times as much fibre and about eight times the effect on the bowel. Wholemeal bread is made from wholemeal flour which is ground wheatgrain which has had none of the bran (the outer husk) removed by the so-called 'refining' process. White flour has had nearly all the bran removed.

Bran on its own is the richest source of fibre but it is rather unpalatable. Bran cereal is much more acceptable but has a rather lower fibre content; however, two dessertspoonfuls will provide an adequate daily fibre intake. Wholewheat breakfast cereals with a high-fibre content are another good source but anyone with a tendency to overweight should eat them without sugar and avoid those containing sugar or honey.

A good way to increase the fibre intake is to base more meals on beans, peas, lentils and other pulses, and use meat more sparingly. Mixtures of different plant foods can provide all the essential amino acids.

Green leafy vegetables, especially spinach, have a fairly high fibre content. Cook them just enough to soften them (preferably steam them) otherwise the nutrients

Fibre Content

Wheat bran (miller's bran) – 44%
Wholemeal flour (unrefined 100% of the grain) – 10%
Wholemeal bread – 9%
Brown bread (wheatmeal) – 5%
White bread – 3%

Bran cereal – 27%
Puffed wheat – 15%
Shredded wheat – 12%
Cornflakes – 11%
Muesli – 7%
Porridge – 1%

Rye crispbread – 12%
Plain digestive biscuits – 6%

Almonds – 14%
Peanuts – 8%

Boiled spinach – 6%
Boiled sprouts – 3%
Boiled cabbage 2%
Boiled carrots – 3%
Boiled potatoes – 1%
Baked potatoes – 3%
Boiled frozen peas – 12%
Boiled fresh peas – 5%
Boiled runner beans – 3%
Baked beans – 7%
Lettuce – 2%

Blackberries – 7%
Bananas – 3%
Pears – 3%
Apples – 2%
Oranges – 2%
Grapefruit – 1%
Tomatoes – 2%

are lost in the cooking water. Fresh fruit and salads, although a good source of vitamins and minerals, are lower down the fibre league. They are regarded as good slimming foods because they are nearly all water, but this makes them less satisfying than the relatively non-fattening, high-fibre 'fillers' such as wholemeal bread and potatoes.

Eat less fat

Leading nutritionists all agree that there is too much fat in most people's diet. In modern developed nations meat has become a staple food to rival bread and potatoes, and nearly 45 per cent of our daily calories come from fat, especially that in meat and dairy products.

There are several reasons why a high-fat diet should be discouraged. Firstly, fat is very high in calories. Weight-for-weight the calorie concentration of butter is about three times that of bread and eight times that of a jacket potato.

Another important reason to be wary of too much fat is its link with heart disease. Research suggests that people with a high level of cholesterol and certain other fatty substances in their blood are more likely to have atheroma (the fatty deposits that silt up the arteries, causing coronary heart disease), and hence a heart attack. Some fats in the diet are thought to increase the level of these 'risk' substances more than others (though not all researchers and scientists are agreed about this). Broadly speaking, fats which contain mainly so-called saturated fatty acids are more likely to raise the risk component, than fats which contain mainly unsaturated fatty acids. Again, broadly speaking, animal fat and dairy products are high in saturated fat, while plant oils and fish oils are usually high in unsaturated fat.

Most nutritionists suggest that the *overall* intake of fatty foods, from whatever source, should be reduced, with a considerable reduction in saturated fats from meat and dairy products. This may mean substituting them to some extent with unsaturated fats. These changes to the diet will not only help in weight control, but may also protect against heart disease and since atheroma starts to silt up the arteries from a surprisingly early age, it is wise to instil a sensible attitude to fatty food before children become too set in their eating habits.

How to reduce fat intake

1. Cut down on butter *and* margarine, but this does not mean you should eat less bread.
2. Eat less meat and remove the visible fat. Even lean steak contains up to 20 per cent fat (chicken has less than half this). Grill meat rather than fry it.
3. Substitute fish for meat. White fish, in particular, is low in fat, and is mainly unsaturated as well. Beware fatty batter, and fat-soaked fried fish fingers.
4. Reduce cream intake, substituting natural yogurt instead. Double dairy cream is nearly half fat. Silver-top milk has less fat than gold-top, and skimmed milk has less still. You do not *have* to drink a pint a day.
5. Cheeses have a high fat content (although they have gained a quite unjustified reputation for being slimming). Only cottage cheese is low in fat (see table).
6. Bear in mind that chocolate, milk or plain, is one-third fat, and that there is also a lot of 'hidden fat' in biscuits and pastries.

Fat in cheese

	Fat Content
Cottage cheese	4%
Cheese spread	23%
Edam type	23%
Camembert type	23%
Processed cheese	25%
Danish Blue type	29%
Cheddar type	34%
Stilton type	40%
Cream cheese	47%

Sugar's 'empty' calories

The sweetness of sugar is an irresistible temptation to millions and we eat an amazing amount in the course of a year. It is not only an essential ingredient of such sweet delights as confectionery, preserves, cakes, pastries, and biscuits, but it is also contained in many drinks and even in savoury sauces and some canned vegetables.

Refined sugar is a highly concentrated source of calories and has virtually *no other nutritional value* – hence the description of sugar as 'empty' calories. It is very easy to eat much more than energy requirements dictate: in order to burn up the energy in four or five lumps of sugar, it would be necessary to walk approximately 1·8 km (1 mile).

The other important factor about sugar is the part it plays in tooth decay. Children who often eat sweet things between meals are likely to acquire a mouthful of fillings. Try to wean children off sweet things with fresh fruit, nuts or cheese.

How to stay slim

Staying slim is almost entirely a question of cutting down on high calorie food, so that overall energy intake does not exceed energy output (see page 50). Exercise to increase the output may help to some extent, but it is surprising how much work has to be done to burn up, say, 300 calories.

Although recent research suggests that regular vigorous exercise readjusts the body's resting metabolic rate so that calories are burnt more efficiently day and night, it is still no substitute for eating fewer calories. It is possible to cut down on calories without having to count them rigorously by following the guidelines that have been stressed repeatedly throughout this chapter: **Eat less fat, Eat less sugar, Eat more fibre.**

To put these principles in terms of the types of food we encounter daily, here is a simplified guide based on the calorie-concentrations of various common food items. If you have a tendency to put on weight you should ration your consumption of foods with a high or medium calorie concentration.

1. **Think very hard before eating any of these high calorie foods:**
sugar, sweets, chocolate, cakes, pastries, biscuits, heavy puddings, honey, syrup, treacle, jam, marmalade, fruit canned in syrup, dried fruit, cream, butter, margarine, lard, cooking oils, meat fat, salad dressing, salad cream, mayonnaise, chips, crisps, roasted peanuts, sweet aperitifs, spirits, liqueurs, most soft drinks and mixers.

2. **Go very carefully with these medium calorie foods:**
fatty meats, bacon, salami, sausages, pâté, eggs, milk, oily fish (like herrings, mackerel, sardines, tuna), all fried foods, cheeses (except cottage cheese), thick creamy soups, nuts, white bread, refined or sugary cereals, rice, refined pasta, beer, cider and wine.

3. **Eat as many of these low calorie foods as you like:**
fresh fruit, salads, green and root vegetables, potatoes, wholemeal bread, wholemeal cereals, bran, white fish, seafood, chicken, rabbit, offal (but these are high in cholesterol), cottage cheese, yoghurt (unsweetened), skimmed milk, clear soups, herbs and spices, low-calorie soft drinks, tea or coffee (no sugar and just a dash of milk), and water.

Remember it is much easier to get yourself into the simple and satisfying routine of staying slim than to force yourself through the purgatory of stomach-rending crash-diets.

The Hidden Addiction

Smoking

Any cigarette smoker will tell you how very pleasant it is to smoke; how it soothes, stimulates or improves the concentration. Some say that it tastes good, it gives them something to do with their hands, makes them look sexy or is a good icebreaker at social gatherings.

Despite all these 'benefits' the great majority of smokers actually want to give it up. The tide has certainly turned against smoking – and for convincing reasons.

Why give up smoking? Firstly, there are the health reasons. Cigarette smoking has been proved, beyond all reasonable doubt, to be the major cause of **lung cancer.** Carcinogens (cancer-causing substances) in the tar can eventually start a growth in the air-tubes, which then invades other tissues. Even moderate cigarette smokers are multiplying their risk of getting lung cancer by up to **25 times** that of a non-smoker.

A much more widespread smoking-related disease is **chronic bronchitis** – a slowly progressive lung condition that develops as a reaction to irritants in the tar of cigarette smoke. The linings of the air-tubes compensate by secreting excessive amounts of mucus (phlegm) which gives rise to the well-known 'smoker's cough'. At the same time the lungs' self-cleaning mechanism is steadily destroyed until eventually, after a period of years, most of the lung tissue is a useless sponge and the victim can hardly rise from his chair without fighting for breath. Chronic bronchitis (and its related disease, emphysema) kills about 30,000 people a year in this country, and many thousands more spend their last dozen or so years as respiratory cripples. Smoker's cough, shortness of breath or frequent clearing of the throat are all signs that the disease is taking hold.

The third main danger from smoking is the part it plays in causing **coronary heart disease** (angina and heart attack). Nicotine and carbon monoxide in cigarette smoke appear to increase the 'silting-up' of the body's arteries. When the arteries supplying the heart get too narrowed, the victim suffers from severe pains in the chest on exertion and if a clot forms he has a heart attack. To make matters worse, carbon monoxide reduces the oxygen-carrying capacity of the blood, and nicotine makes the oxygen-starved heart beat irregularly. The average smoker is twice as likely to die from heart disease as the non-smoker.

Smoking is particularly dangerous for women on the contraceptive pill, especially if they are over the age of about 35. The combined effect of oestrogen in the pill and substances in cigarette smoke significantly increases the risk of thrombosis.

These are the main health hazards to the cigarette smoker and there is a long list of others. On average, a cigarette smoker shortens his life by **5½ minutes for each cigarette smoked.**

It is not just the smoker's health which is affected. Pregnant women who smoke, especially during the second half of pregnancy, greatly increase the risk of miscarriage or stillbirth and are also gambling with the mental and physical health of their baby.

If you are a smoker you will notice instant differences when you give up. Your heart and lungs will start to work more efficiently and your blood will carry more oxygen, so you will be less breathless when you exert yourself and have more stamina and staying power. Also, your resistance to coughs, colds and several other illnesses will improve. Your sense of taste will be enhanced and you will save quite a lot of money.

How to give up smoking

There is no easy way to give up smoking. For most, it is a struggle, requiring considerable self-control and determination. Unless you are convinced that you really mean to quit smoking, your attempt will fail.

It helps to have a strategy for giving up. One way is to decide about a week in advance which day you will actually quit (Q-day). Make a note in your diary and tell everyone about it. You may even manage to persuade a workmate, friend or someone in the family to give up with you.

For a few typical working days beforehand you should restrict yourself firmly to only those cigarettes you really *need* to smoke. A good idea is to keep a smoking diary of these 'necessary' cigarettes, noting the time you lit up and what you were doing. This will be useful later when it comes to devising tactics for fighting off temptation.

The night before Q-day, ceremoniously light up for the last time and throw or give away any remaining cigarettes. Remind yourself again of the benefits of stopping and tell yourself that tomorrow you will be a non-smoker (despite your craving for a cigarette!).

Q-day

Study your smoking diary and decide how to cope with today's difficult situations. Try to think of ways to break routines, to distract or

1. Smoke only two thirds of the cigarette – much of the harmful tar and nicotine collects in the final third.

2. Switch to filter cigarettes and a lower tar brand.

3. Make smoking a little more difficult for yourself. Buy just one packet at a time and make it ten rather than twenty. Hide your lighter, or matches, or leave them at home.

4. Do not smoke out of doors, in bed or in front of children.

5. Do not accept cigarettes from others.

6. Sit in no-smoking areas of public transport, restaurants and cinemas.

7. When you reach for a cigarette, stop, look at your watch and wait five minutes before taking it out of the packet.

8. Cut out your two least favourite cigarettes of the day. Each week cut out two more.

comfort yourself. Do not think of tomorrow, just think about getting through today. These hints may help you:

– If you miss something in your mouth, try substitutes such as chewing gum.

– If you feel awkward without a cigarette to occupy your hands, find something to play with: coins, biro, a bunch of keys.

– If you start to get tense, try a simple relaxation technique. Breathe all the way in; hold it for a few seconds, really stretching your lungs, and then breathe all the way out. Repeat this ten times, preferably in a smoke-free atmosphere.

Do whatever you can to change your daily routine so that you are not being tempted constantly. If you enjoyed a cigarette with a cup of tea or coffee, try switching to fresh orange juice or hot soup.

Keep away from places where people are smoking, pubs and canteens for example, and sit in no-smoking railway compartments.

If you tended to smoke when you were relaxing, keep yourself busy with a variety of practical activities, and spend as much time in the open air as possible.

Start saving the money that smoking would have cost you and plan a treat for yourself at the end of your first month as a non-smoker.

The days following

Take each day as it comes and do not worry about facing the rest of your life without cigarettes. Keep reminding yourself why you have stopped smoking and try to invent new ways of coping with difficulties you encountered the previous day.

The first two or three weeks are usually the worst, but many ex-smokers find that after a few days things get much easier.

Some ex-smokers have an increased appetite and tend to put on weight. This is a temporary change brought about partly by an alteration in the body's metabolism and partly by the need for something to put in your mouth. In a few weeks your appetite will re-adjust and your weight will return to normal.

If you can't give up, cut down on smoking

Research has shown that in the long-run it is generally not as easy to cut down as it is to give up suddenly and completely. However you may find that it suits you better. It does reduce the shock to the system of sudden nicotine withdrawal.

Other ways of cutting down which are effective for about one in every three smokers include:

Special tablets and filters to reduce the nicotine-dependence. Nicotine containing chewing-gum which may reduce the need to smoke, in people who are heavily nicotine-dependent.

Smoking withdrawal groups. These are groups of smokers giving up with the help of a counsellor trained to guide them. To find one in your area check with your local health authority.

Hypnosis. This does work for some smokers, but only by providing a boost to the willpower of those who really want to stop.

Cigars and pipes Generally speaking these are much less hazardous to health and fitness than cigarettes, **providing the smoke is not inhaled.** Cigar and pipe-smoking multiply the chances of contracting mouth and throat cancer by up to ten times, but the overall risk of ill-health is far lower than that caused by cigarette smoking.

Alcohol

For some people 'having a drink' means indulging in an occasional sherry while for others it means whole evenings, and most of the following days, spent in a state of intoxication. For the great majority who take alcohol in moderation, drinking appears to be a pleasurable and relatively harmless way of fostering informality, hospitality and friendship.

But is alcohol really so harmless? Even for normal 'social' drinkers?

Alcohol-related problems have rocketed in the UK in the past ten years. Drinking and driving offences have more than doubled and convictions for drunkenness have increased by more than half. Hospital treatment for alcohol-dependence has doubled and deaths from the long term effects of alcohol have trebled.

Of course there is considerable variation in precise alcohol content, but as a rough guide: 280ml (half pint) of beer equals one normal glass of table wine equals one normal glass of sherry equals one single measure of spirits.

The Alcohol in Drinks	
Spirits (70% proof) (whisky, gin, brandy)	40% alcohol
Fortified wines (sherry, madeira, port)	20% alcohol
Table wines	10% alcohol
Beers	5% alcohol

The effect of alcohol

Alcohol is absorbed very rapidly into the bloodstream, mostly through the stomach wall. Within minutes it reaches the brain where it acts as a depressant of normal function. The effect it has depends on the blood alcohol level, which depends on how much is drunk, how quickly it is absorbed, how quickly the liver can detoxify it, and the weight of the person concerned.

The first faculty to be affected by alcohol is the ability to judge the speed and distance of moving objects accurately. This occurs after as little as 560 ml (one pint) of beer (equivalent to a blood alcohol level of 30 mg per 100 ml). After another 840 ml (one-and-a-half pints) the individual's chances of having a driving accident would be four times greater and his blood alcohol would be about 80 mg per 100 ml – the legal limit allowed for driving. With twice as much (160 mg per 100 ml), he would be losing self-control, his speech would be slurred and he would be excitable. The chances of an accident are now up to 25 times greater. From there, his condition would degenerate with progressive drinks, until at a blood level of 400 mg per 100 ml, he would slip into a coma. A bottle of spirits (500 mg per 100 ml) can cause death.

The absorption of alcohol into the bloodstream can be delayed by having food in the stomach, especially fatty food. The liver 'burns up' the alcohol at a rate equivalent to 280 ml (half-pint) of beer an hour. After drinking about three litres (6 pints) at night a person could still be over the legal limit to drive the **next morning.**

Sensible Drinking

With a little care it is easy to enjoy the pleasures of alcohol without falling prey to the drawbacks. Arrange for transport home if you will be drinking more than about two pints of beer, four glasses of wine or two doubles of spirits. Line your stomach with a snack or a drink of milk before you start drinking and set a limit to the number of drinks you want, and try not to be persuaded to exceed it.

Never feel you have to choose an alcoholic drink, or force someone else to have one. Beware the sly 'topper-upper' who fills your glass without you realizing it, or a fruit punch that tastes innocuous but is actually loaded with alcohol. Always dilute spirits with plenty of non-alcoholic mixers and sip drinks slowly.

Hangovers

One could be forgiven for thinking that a hangover is some sort of divine retribution for a night of alcoholic revelry. In fact, the headache, depression, queasiness and jangled nerves of a hangover are due to changes in the chemistry of the brain brought on partly by the alcohol itself and partly by the many other substances present in most drinks.

Alcohol is a 'diuretic' – it causes more water to be passed in the urine, and so it has a

Hangover Index

	Congener Level
Brandy	6
Red wine	6
Rum	5
Sherry	5
Whisky	3
Beer	3
White wine	2
Gin	2
Vodka	1

The 'Slippery-Slope' Checklist

Do you often drink alone?

Do you often have a drink before lunchtime?

Do you usually drink for its effect on your mood?

Do your weekday afternoons often seem a bit of a blur?

Do you find a drink or two helps you to face difficult problems?

Do you find other people are slow at drinking up and buying the next round?

If you answer 'yes' to any of these, it could mean that you are developing a dependence on alcohol which might soon give you problems. If you feel you are beginning to rely too much on drink, talk the problem over with someone who may be able to advise or help you. This may be a member of the family, a friend at work, your doctor, or a counselling service (you do not have to be an 'alcoholic' to seek advice).

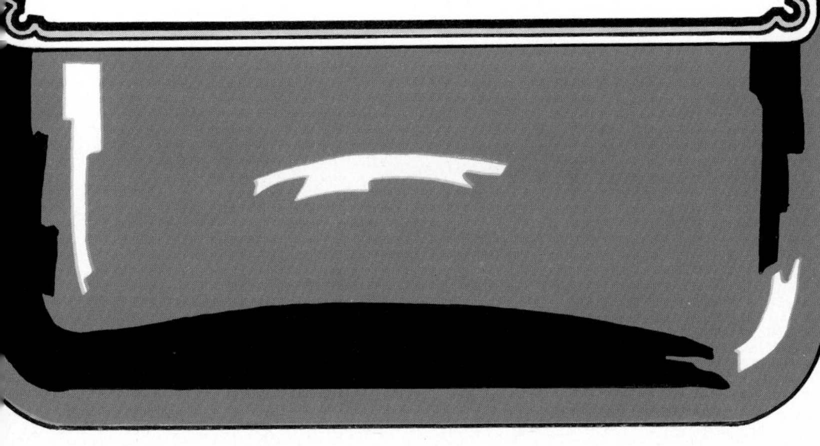

dehydrating effect. This in itself can cause headaches and nausea. Most drinks contain other substances which provide characteristic colour and flavour. These are usually organic compounds and are called 'congeners'. Recent research has shown that they are at least partly to blame for hangovers; the more congeners, the worse the hangover. Some drinks have more congeners than others, see chart (left).

The liver slowly but steadily removes alcohol and congeners from the bloodstream and hence the brain, so coping with a hangover is mainly a question of waiting for the liver to detoxify the system.

To prevent a hangover

1. Drink less alcohol.
2. Choose weaker drinks, preferably with plenty of 'mixers' to combat dehydration.
3. Pick drinks with a low hangover index (see chart).
4. Drink half a litre (*one pint*) of water before you go to sleep.

On waking with a sore head:

1. Drink plenty of water or fresh orange juice.
2. Take two paracetamol tablets for the headache (*not* aspirin which may irritate the stomach even more than the alcohol).
3. A cup of strong tea or coffee will act as a reviver.

Alcoholism

In simple terms, an alcoholic is someone whose repeated drinking has led to (or is leading to) interference with personal relationships, work, family life, or mental or physical health.

The image of the alcoholic as a red-nosed, hiccoughing drunk is very misleading because the majority of alcoholics are still in the early stages of the disorder and appear quite normal to the casual observer. More often than not it takes a close friend, or someone in the family to notice that something is wrong and that drinking is at least partly to blame. If a drinking habit is causing problems then the drinker needs some sort of help.

The dividing line between being a 'social' drinker, whose drinking is under control, and a 'problem' drinker, is a blurred one. The experts generally agree that anyone who regularly drinks more than 2 litres (four pints) of beer a day (or four doubles of spirits, or one bottle of wine) is running a high risk of developing a serious drink problem.

Caffeine – tea and coffee

Tea and coffee are 'pick-me-ups'. They contain a mild stimulant drug called caffeine which acts directly on the brain, speeding thought processes, shortening reaction times, and relieving fatigue. It can also combat physical tiredness.

The other effects of caffeine are less welcome. It increases the production of urine, raises the pulse rate, and – if taken to excess – can cause restlessness, agitation, palpitations and trembling. Too much tea or coffee can therefore cause tension and nervousness. How much is too much depends on individual body chemistry – just one cup of strong coffee is enough to upset some people whilst others can drink cup after cup with impunity. As a rough guide, adverse reactions usually occur if an individual has more than about 300 mg of caffeine within a few hours. A cup of brewed coffee contains 100–150 mg of caffeine; instant coffee, 75–100 mg; tea, 60–75 mg. (Incidentally, a bottle of cola contains 40–60 mg of caffeine, and even a cup of cocoa contains 20–50 mg.)

For those who are sensitive to caffeine a bed-time drink can interfere with sleep. Because caffeine stimulates the stomach to produce acid, tea and coffee should be avoided by indigestion or peptic ulcer sufferers unless taken with plenty of milk or food. High doses of caffeine can cause palpitations (irregular heartbeat) and it is unwise for people who have heart trouble to drink strong tea or coffee.

Painkillers

The vast majority of the 5,000,000,000 analgesic tablets (pain-killers) swallowed in the UK each year are bought over the counter without a doctor's prescription. There are dozens of different products, but they nearly all contain one, or a combination, of the following three active ingredients:

Aspirin – (acetyl salicylic acid). This effectively relieves mild to moderate pain, reduces fever and inflammation and is non-habit-forming. Its main disadvantage is that it can irritate the stomach lining and may cause gastric bleeding, so it should not be used for a stomach upset. Ordinary aspirin is best taken crushed, with a glass of milk to soothe irritation. Soluble aspirin is quicker acting and is also kinder to the stomach.

It is important never to take more than the recommended dose. A heavy overdose of aspirin causes ringing in the ears, gasping, nausea, mental confusion and may lead eventually to coma and death. Aspirin poisoning is a real hazard for small children, especially toddlers. Aspirin (and paracetamol) must now by law, be sold in child-resistant containers. Even so, they should be kept out of reach.

Many people are sensitive to aspirin, which brings them out in a rash or gives them an attack of wheezing. They should take a paracetamol-based analgesic.

Paracetamol – Paracetamol reduces fever but, unlike aspirin, does not relieve inflammation, and is therefore not so effective for conditions like arthritis. It does not irritate the stomach lining and is therefore more suitable in cases where pain is accompanied by gastric discomfort such as a hangover. Like any pain killer, it is dangerous in overdosage and will irreversibly damage the liver before other symptoms appear. Long term use of high doses can impair kidney function. Keep all paracetamol-containing medicines and pills well away from children.

Codeine – This is a rather stronger pain-killer than aspirin or paracetamol, but it does not reduce fever or inflammation. It is often included in aspirin-based or paracetamol-based products. An overdose of codeine causes constipation, drowsiness and respiratory failure.

Most of us take our everyday drugs for granted: but they can cause problems.

Antacids

These are preparations which neutralize the acid in the stomach and thus give relief from some forms of gastric discomfort, notably pain from peptic ulcers. They are often taken for the wrong reasons, the only *proper* use for antacids being to relieve the pain caused by an irritated gullet or stomach, usually felt beneath the breastbone ('heartburn') or in the upper abdomen ('indigestion'). There are many causes of such irritation, ranging from dietary indiscretions to peptic ulcers, but all are aggravated by the normal acidity of the stomach juice and are temporarily relieved by neutralizing it.

Generally speaking, liquid preparations (including powders that are mixed with water) are more effective than tablets, although tablets can be carried about more conveniently. All antacid preparations are intended to be used between meals, but remember that food itself is usually antacid and that milk is a very effective neutralizer.

There are many different antacid preparations available without prescription. There are two main types:

Short-acting – These work quickly but fade quickly and, because they are absorbed into the bloodstream, may upset the body's chemical balance with prolonged use. Sodium bicarbonate is an example and is found in well-known seltzers. Calcium carbonate is another fast and effective antacid, but can be constipating and, if taken together with milk over a long period, can cause calcium poisoning.

Long-acting – These take longer to work, but are effective for longer because they are less quickly absorbed into the bloodstream. Those containing magnesium salts may cause diarrhoea.

Laxatives

These are medicines for relieving constipation and are often taken unnecessarily by people who are not actually constipated. Normal bowel habits vary considerably – two or three movements a day being normal for some people, and about once a week for others. True constipation means that the stools are passed so infrequently that they become uncomfortably hard and difficult to pass.

For most people, constipation can be prevented by eating food containing plenty of 'fibre' or roughage (see page 26). This provides natural bulk and keeps the stools soft and shifting along. However, if constipation does become a problem, a mild laxative can help. There are three main types:

'Bulk' laxatives – These work by temporarily increasing the bulk of the stool by absorbing water. They are particularly useful for elderly people with poor appetites. Examples are Epsom salts and psyllium seeds.

'Stimulant' laxatives – These work by stimulating the large intestine (colon) to contract thereby pushing its contents along and producing the desire to defecate. Some forms are taken by mouth, and take several hours to work, others by suppository pushed through the anus into the rectum, and work within half-an-hour. Because they irritate the bowel, these preparations can cause colic or gripes and should not be used on more than an occasional basis. Examples are senna cascara and castor oil.

'Lubricant' laxatives – These work by softening and lubricating the hard stools making them easier to pass. They should not be taken over a long period since they may interfere with vitamin absorption.

They are most suitable for constipation after childbirth, for those suffering from piles or any other condition that makes defecation painful.

Liquid paraffin (medicinal, *not* the fuel) is the best known example.

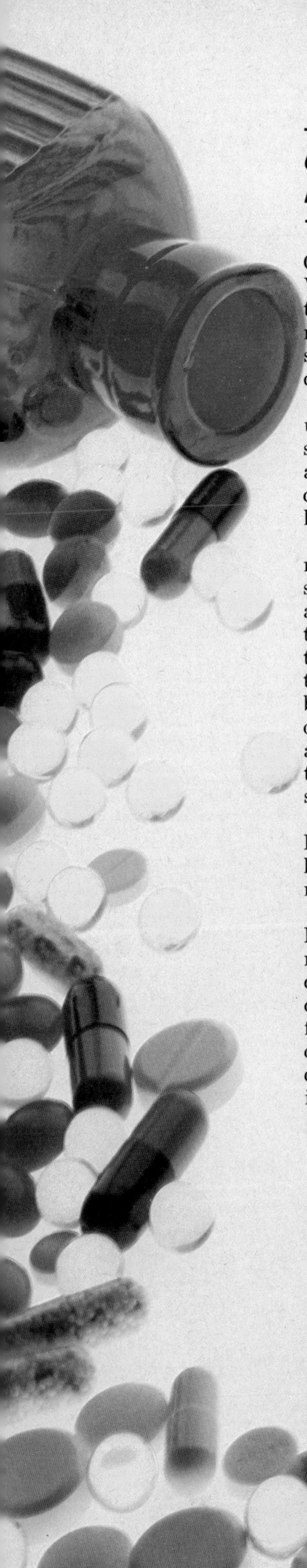

Cold remedies and cough mixtures

Colds and influenza are caused by viruses. Viruses do not respond to antibiotics and there is no effective 'cure' for either the common cold or 'flu. The best you can hope for is some relief of the symptoms whilst your body defence system overcomes the infection.

There is no point in seeing the doctor unless the infection is causing earache, sinusitis, or a prolonged chesty cough lasting at least a week. The doctor should however be consulted if the sufferer is frail or has a weak heart or chest condition.

Proprietary 'cold remedies', containing a mixture of drugs to alleviate some of the symptoms outlined below are now widely available without prescription. However, they are quite expensive and no more effective than the individual ingredients. Mixtures intended to be taken at night should not be taken by day unless you are able to 'sleep it off'. They usually contain antihistamine and alcohol, which cause drowsiness. 'Day' mixtures, on the other hand, usually contain the stimulant caffeine.

Headache, sore throat, aching neck or limbs – relieved by pain killers such as aspirin and paracetamol (see page 36).

Runny or stuffy nose and sinuses – relieved by decongestants (such as ephedrine, or phenylephrine) which temporarily dry up nasal secretions. These may be in the form of nose drops, nasal sprays or inhalants, or in mixtures to be taken by mouth. Nose drops and nasal sprays may damage the lining of the nose if used repeatedly and they are certainly best avoided in babies and young children.

Nasal decongestants taken by mouth are included in many cold remedies. However, because they are absorbed into the bloodstream they can cause side effects such as drowsiness.

Fever – reduced by aspirin and paracetamol taken with plenty of fluids.

Cough – This is caused by irritation of the throat, windpipe (trachea) or the bronchial tubes in the lungs. There are two main types of cough mixture, each dealing with one of the two types of cough.

A dry irritating cough does not bring up phlegm but generally keeps the sufferer awake at night. It can be calmed with a cough suppressant mixture. Do not exceed the stated dose as an overdose of cough suppressant may also suppress the breathing reflex.

A chesty cough with phlegm can be helped with steam inhalations (head under towel over a bowl of steaming water, with or without menthol crystals).

Expectorant cough mixtures are designed to loosen the phlegm and help the sufferer cough it up. Expectorant mixtures are also useful for people with chronic (long-lasting) chesty coughs.

Sore throat – Most sore throats are caused by viruses and are not helped by antibiotics. Aspirin or paracetamol will take the edge off the pain and throat pastilles may help a little by stimulating the nose and throat lining to secrete mucus, which has a soothing and lubricating effect on the inflamed throat. Gargles have a similar action. If sore throat persists for more than a week, or if the tonsils seem inflamed and coated with a yellow substance, or if there is earache, see the doctor.

Vitamin C

Some research has suggested that very large doses of vitamin C may minimize the symptoms and shorten the duration of a cold if taken as soon as it begins. However, most of the evidence does not support this conclusion.

Tranquillizers and Hypnotics

In the UK prescriptions for tranquillizers are being issued at the rate of nearly 22,000,000 a year – and at the rate of 17,000,000 for hypnotics (sleeping pills). These drugs are potentially addictive.

Tranquillizers are prescribed for anxiety symptoms and 'nerves', often for premenstrual tension or menopausal anxiety. Tranquillizers are not just calming – they also interfere with coordination, can cause drowsiness and greatly increase the depressant effect of alcohol. Despite popular belief, it is possible to become physically, as well as psychologically, dependent on tranquillizers.

The majority of prescribed hypnotics used

to be barbiturates. These are sedatives which, if taken at night, can induce sleep. However, they are quite definitely addictive and can cause unpleasant withdrawal symptoms if stopped suddenly. Because of their frequent misuse and the danger of accidental death when taken with alcohol, doctors are reluctant to prescribe them nowadays.

There are many different types of *non*-barbiturate hypnotics that are prescribed. Most of these have the same disadvantages as tranquillizers.

Whilst hypnotics may induce a full night's sleep, the quality of that sleep is not as restful as normal sleep (see page 46). Most prescriptions for tranquillizers and hynotics are unnecessary and more attention should be paid to dealing with the root cause of the problem.

Illegal Drugs

Cannabis

(*alias* marijuana, 'pot', 'dope', 'hash', 'grass')
The active ingredient is obtained from a plant resin which is usually smoked with tobacco in what is known as a 'joint'. The temporary effect of cannabis is to produce a state of benign relaxation, a feeling of well-being and an enhanced appreciation of some sensory stimuli (particularly music). However, it also reduces alertness and coordination, and causes muscular weakness. It has a strong sedative action if taken in excess or with alcohol and driving under the influence of cannabis is hazardous. It is likely that occasional use is fairly harmless, but considerable debate rages over the long-term dangers. There are fears that heavy use could have possible long-term effects on memory, fertility and the immune system.

Cannabis is not physically addictive in the way cigarettes and alcohol can be. There are no physical withdrawal symptoms – but it can produce a state of psychological dependence. There is also no indisputable evidence that the use of cannabis will tend to lead to hard drugs like heroin.

Amphetamines

(*alias* 'Speed')
These drugs, related to adrenaline, were once widely prescribed as 'pep pills' for mental lassitude and lethargy. They have a powerful mental stimulant action and were thought to be helpful in states of depression, such as menopausal 'blues'. They also suppress the appetite and were used as an aid to slimming.

Unfortunately they not only cause mental agitation if taken in excess, but also lead to drug dependence, higher and higher doses being needed to achieve the effect. In the late 'sixties, they were widely abused by young people who took huge doses for a 'speed trip'. Some users injected amphetamines intravenously with disastrous results. Once the dangers of amphetamines were apparent the drugs came under strict control and are now seldom prescribed, although there is a thriving black market in them.

Pills for peace of mind. Every year Britain's doctors issue about 40 million prescriptions for tranquillizers and sleeping pills. Have a periodic check and throw out any pills that you no longer need.

Cocaine

(*alias* 'Coke', 'snow')
Originally used as a local anaesthetic, cocaine has been a drug of addiction for about a century. It has similar temporary effects to amphetamines producing a sensation of cheerful alertness and, in higher doses, anxiety and hallucinations.

Habitual cocaine users have to take bigger and bigger doses of the drug to get the 'kick' and develop a strong psychological craving for it. Long term use causes loss of weight, loss of memory and personality.

LSD

Lysergic acid diethylamide
(*alias* 'Acid')
LSD is a hallucinogenic drug – producing mental illusions of a mainly visual nature known as an 'acid trip'. Its precise effect depends on the user's mental and physical state (in particular whether he is comfortable, relaxed and happy, or edgy, irritable and anxious). LSD tends to grossly magnify mood and to conjure up psychedelic fantasies to match it.

In the short term LSD can lead to accidents under the influence and also trigger off severe mental breakdown. It is seldom taken on a long-term basis and is not addictive.

Heroin

Diamorphine
Heroin is a narcotic drug related to morphine and used medically for the occasional relief of sudden severe pain (such as a coronary), in which situation it is not addictive. However, in non-medical use, the drug has become society's most dangerous drug of dependence.

Users are attracted to it by its initial euphoriant effect, but it is powerfully physically addictive. After a few doses, withdrawal causes horribly unpleasant symptoms and addicts soon find themselves needing bigger and bigger doses, more and more frequently just to stave off the accompanying horrors.

In their hurry to inject themselves, heroin addicts often use unsterile syringes and needles resulting in sores, abscesses, hepatitis and septicaemia.

Overdoses are fatal.

Taking the Strain

How to avoid stress

The health aspects of stress have been the subject of considerable research over the last 30 years, particularly the way it may give rise to a variety of physical ailments. Our bodies respond to stressful situations by preparing for 'flight or fight'. Adrenaline hormones are released into the bloodstream, instantly increasing the heartrate and the supply of oxygen to the muscles, and the body is alert and ready for rapid action. In most situations, however, social convention forces us to repress instinctive behaviour. Many stress-induced illnesses may be the result of 'bottling up' the fight or flight response, including, in the long term, peptic ulcers, high blood pressure and heart disease.

How to relax

Short of becoming a total recluse, there is no easy way for most people to avoid stress altogether, but there are a million and one different ways of relaxing. Some involve literally relaxing one's mind and body – lying in a warm bath or listening to soothing music. For people who get tense if they 'do nothing', relaxing might mean following a more active pursuit. Satisfaction and pleasure are the key to relaxation, which means, too, that a satisfying sex life plays an important part in helping to soothe mind and body, thereby contributing to the harmony of family life.

Everyday ways of relaxing are vital in combating the long-term effects of stress and time *must* be set aside for them. They are *not* a waste of time as some 'workaholics' maintain. Some people however, just cannot relax even when they try to distract themselves. It is possible that they simply do not know *how* to relax and may, therefore, find it helps to try one of several relaxation techniques.

In the same way that it is possible to become tense and nervous by just *imagining* some awful threat, it is quite possible to react in the opposite way and to feel relaxed and easy, by imagining something soothing and tranquil.

When you are feeling tense and worried, find a few minutes to go somewhere where you know you will not be disturbed. Sit down, close your eyes and try to relax your muscles. Now imagine a scene which conjures up feelings of peace and tranquillity in you – a special place in the countryside or an empty, sun-drenched beach. Imagine the whole scene in detail and imagine yourself there, lying back and relaxing, listening to the birds or the waves on the shore. Wallow in the scene for several minutes, then open your eyes. Many people find this a very effective way to relax in the middle of a busy day.

Deep breathing

In many situations of tension or anxiety, the natural reaction is to take short, panting breaths with the upper part of the chest. This keeps the lungs full of air, so they are prepared for a sudden burst of activity. By contrast in a relaxed state, it is usual to take slow breaths using the abdominal muscles (watch someone breathing whilst they are asleep). Deep 'abdominal' breathing is an excellent way to relieve tension and is often taught in yoga and meditation classes.

To practise it, lie down on your back, or sit back in an easy chair, with knees half-bent, in a quiet place. Place your hands on your abdomen so that your fingertips are touching midway between your ribcage and your waist. Lie quietly for a minute or two, breathing softly and gently. You will feel your tummy expand a little as you breathe in, separating your fingertips. Do not force the breathing-in, otherwise the ribcage expands with the muscles of the upper chest. Simply breathe quietly. The breathing is being performed by the diaphragm, the internal sheet of muscle which separates the chest from the abdomen. As the diaphragm contracts it pulls air into the chest and bulges the tummy. Watch and feel this happening, and then gradually increase the depth of breathing, all the time using only the diaphragm, not the chest. Make the breaths deeper and slower, concentrating on the air flowing smoothly in and smoothly out. Keep this going for as long as you have time to spare.

Tension-relaxation exercises

This technique works on the principle that you more readily learn the sensation of relaxing any particular muscle group (such as those in the neck, shoulders, hands, etc) if you first experience the sensation of systematically tensing it. Begin by tensing each muscle group throughout your body for a few seconds, until you really feel the tension. Then relax and concentrate on the sensation of the tension draining away.

Again, find a quiet undisturbed spot where you can sit or lie down comfortably. Place your legs slightly apart and your arms a little away from your sides. Close your eyes. Begin with six deep breaths. Keeping your legs straight, pull the toes of both feet towards your head, thus tensing the muscles at the front of the calves. Feel the tension and then relax. Let the tension drain away. Now

Back massage soothes away the tensions of the day. The basic routine includes firm strokes with the flats of the hands (1), deep rotary pressure (2), lighter strokes with the fingertips (3) and slapping or pounding with the palms (4).

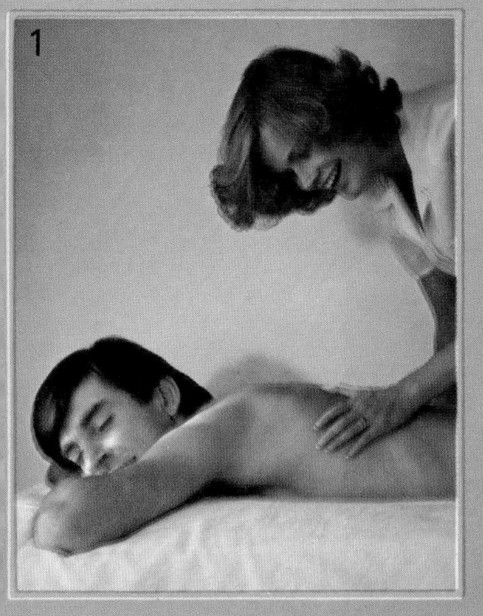

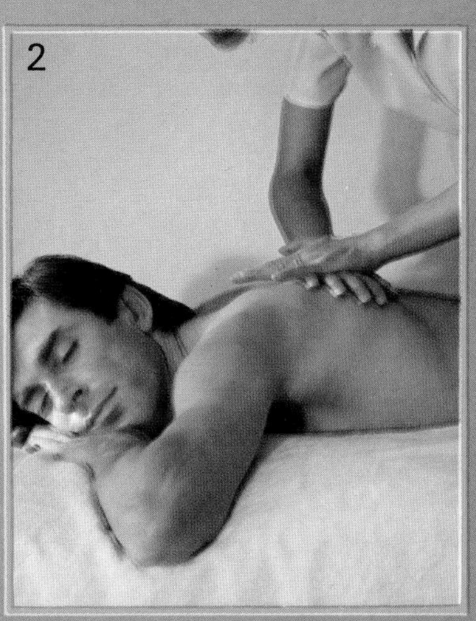

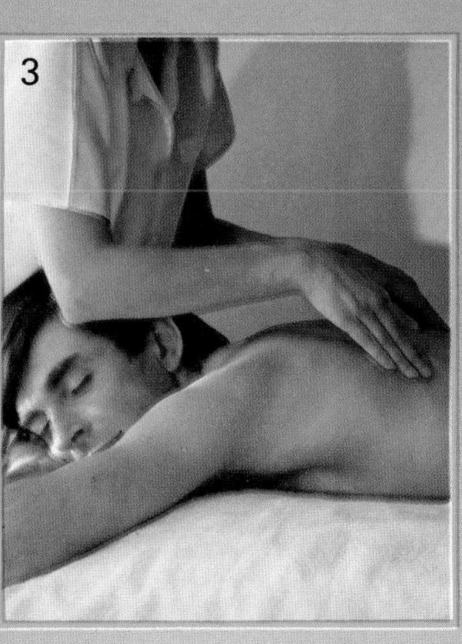

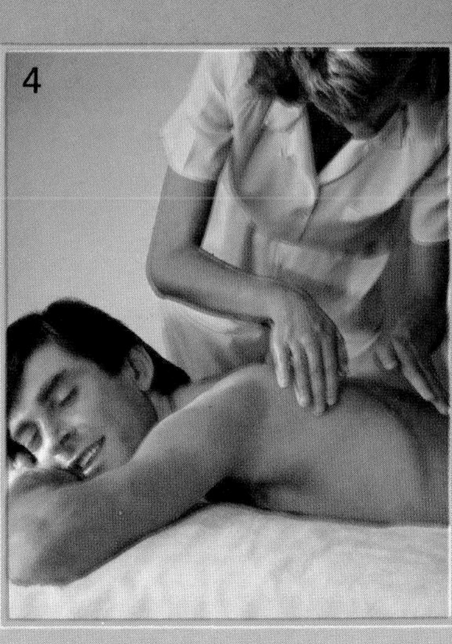

push your feet away from your head, tightening the rear calf muscles. Feel the tension and then relax it away. Repeat this process with the thigh muscles. Then go through the same routine in your arms by first clenching both fists and relaxing, and then tightening your shoulders and relaxing. Then your neck. Force your head backwards against the floor, feel the tension and then relax. Screw your face up into a tight wince, as if someone was just about to burst a balloon right in front of your nose. Hold the tension for about 30 seconds and then relax it away. Finally, lie still for as many minutes as you can spare, relaxing your whole body and feeling the sensation of the muscles relaxing.

Massage

Tense muscles knot into tender trigger points. Waste products produced by contracting muscle fibres accumulate and irritate nerve endings, causing an aching discomfort, which leads to still more tension.

As sufferers from muscle cramp will know, a good way to release the spasm is to stretch the muscle. The same principle is used in both massage and yoga. In yoga, long, slow, stretches along the line of action are used to relax the body's musculature, whereas with massage very localized and more rapid stretching is used by pushing muscles across their line of action.

The muscles most responsive to massage are those that are rigid and static most of the day, such as the muscles at the back of the head and neck and those across the back of the shoulders and down the back of the trunk. These are difficult to reach yourself so it is necessary to get someone to massage them for you.

Lie face down in a warm room, preferably after a warm bath and preferably naked, or sit on a chair and rest your arms on a table in front of you. Your partner should sit in a position where he or she can apply equal pressure symmetrically on both sides of your spine. A little talc or baby oil helps to lubricate the skin.

There are many different techniques practised in massage. Some involve firm smooth strokes with the flats of the hands or thumbs, others use deep rotary pressure with the heels of the hands, others employ the knuckles or fingertips, while still others use vigorous rapid clapping or pounding movements with the flats or sides of the hands. Firm stroking and deep kneading movements are particularly relaxing whereas a light touch should be avoided because it tickles and tenses. It is best to work symmetrically down both sides of the spine, altogether spending about 30 minutes.

Meditation

If the thought of meditation conjures up visions of weird Eastern practices or pot-smoking flower-children, then it may be a revelation to you to learn that most people experience trance-like states similar to meditation surprisingly frequently. In its very simplest form, meditation is allowing the mind to be lulled by a simple repetitive sensation—a fountain, waterfall, waves on a beach or even the action and sound of machinery. If one concentrates entirely on this repetitive sensation, ridding the mind of all other thoughts, one soon becomes lulled into a relaxed state. The mind 'locks-on' to the repetitive stimulus with the effect that other possibly more urgent or anxiety provoking thoughts get crowded out.

Meditation as such, is based on the same principle of blotting out distracting thoughts by giving the mind something simple and repetitive on which to concentrate. This is sometimes called a 'mantra' and it consists quite simply of a single word or sound or utterance which is repeated over and over and over again either in the head or out loud. Words which contain either a humming sound or a hissing sound seem to be most effective.

To meditate, sit comfortably, in a quiet room, with no distractions. Close your eyes; try to relax; do some deep breathing. Start repeating your mantra over again and again, concentrating on the *sound* of the word, not the spelling. Think about nothing but that sound. If you get distracted, just start again. After a while you will find it easier and easier to concentrate your mind on the mantra and banish your anxious thoughts.

Ten-minute meditations like this can soothe the arousal centre in your brain and leave you feeling refreshed and relaxed.

Yoga

The practice of yoga began in India some 3,000 years ago and it is only in the past few years that it has spread widely to other parts of the world. Now evening classes in yoga are among the most popular in the local adult education curriculum and they attract a wide spectrum of people of both sexes and all ages, including many retired people.

Yoga in the fullest meaning of the word, is a philosophical and practical discipline embracing the spiritual moral, mental and physical fulfilment of the devotee. However,

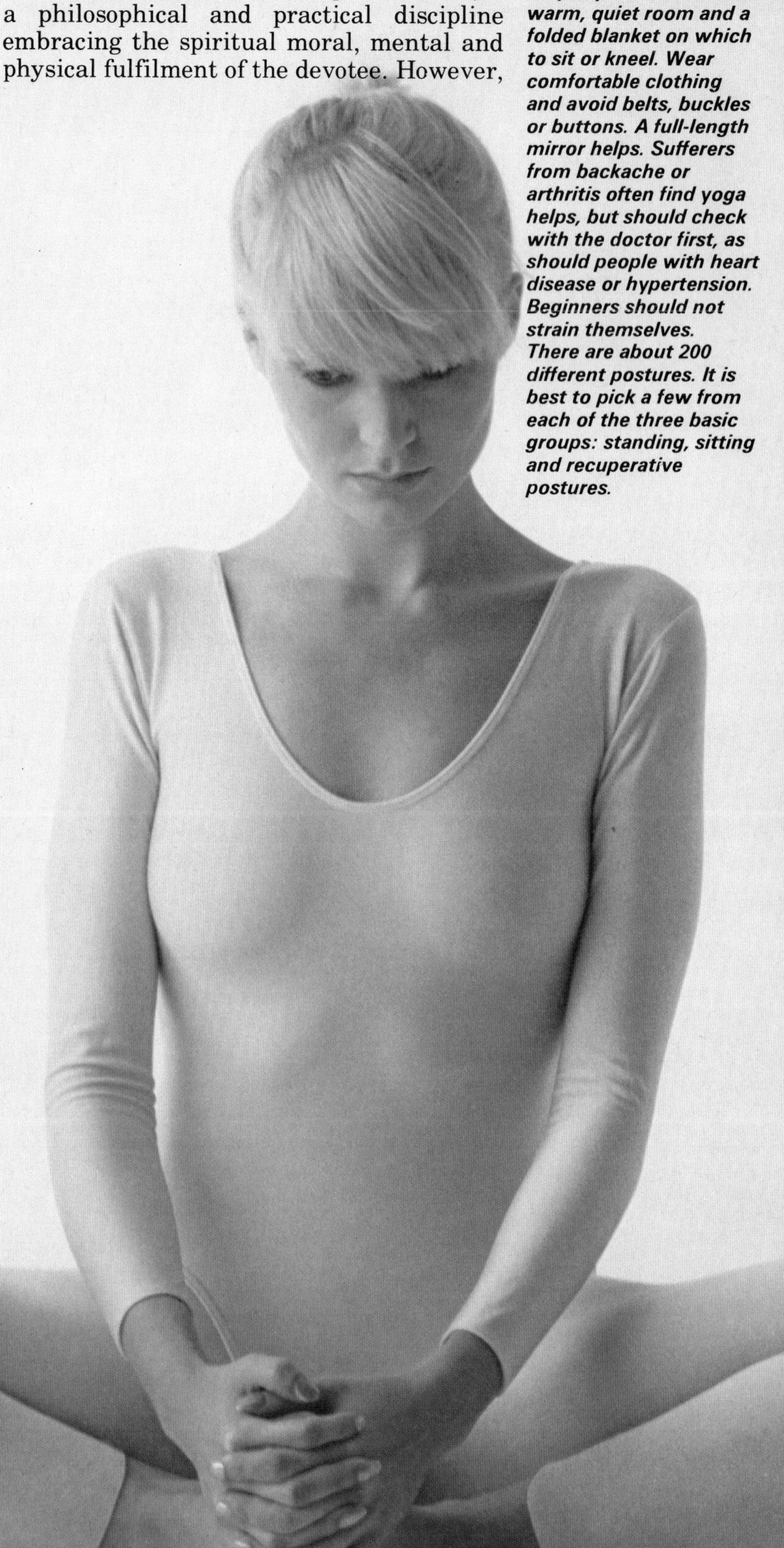

You can learn yoga without attending classes. There are several excellent books on the subject and the only requirements are a warm, quiet room and a folded blanket on which to sit or kneel. Wear comfortable clothing and avoid belts, buckles or buttons. A full-length mirror helps. Sufferers from backache or arthritis often find yoga helps, but should check with the doctor first, as should people with heart disease or hypertension. Beginners should not strain themselves. There are about 200 different postures. It is best to pick a few from each of the three basic groups: standing, sitting and recuperative postures.

the more limited form that is most widely practised is known as hatha yoga and consists mainly of a series of physical and mental exercises which refresh the mind and relax the body. The exercises mostly take the form of a series of postures, which are carried out slowly and deliberately, the emphasis being on muscle control and joint suppleness.

While some improvement in strength might follow regular yoga exercises, there is no rapid movement, so they have no effect on enhancing stamina. Full control and balance, however, require considerable study and practice and at a later stage the techniques of deep breathing and meditation are included in the teaching. The effect of this discipline of mind and body is to impart a feeling of physical vigour and inner calm.

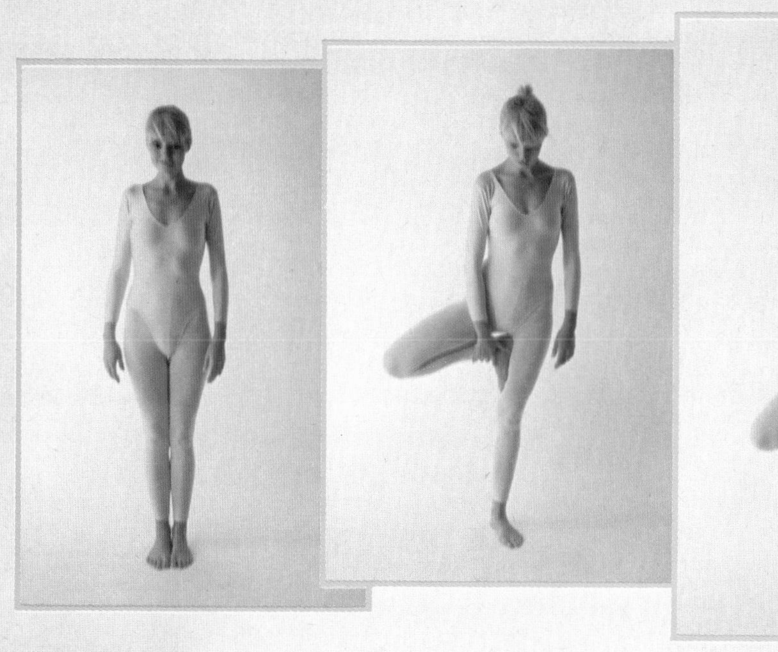
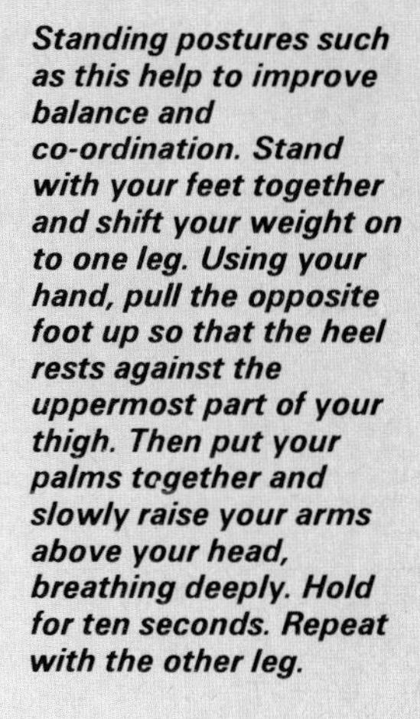

Standing postures such as this help to improve balance and co-ordination. Stand with your feet together and shift your weight on to one leg. Using your hand, pull the opposite foot up so that the heel rests against the uppermost part of your thigh. Then put your palms together and slowly raise your arms above your head, breathing deeply. Hold for ten seconds. Repeat with the other leg.

A recuperative posture to keep your spine supple. Lie on your back with your arms stretched out to either side and your legs together. Raise both legs slowly until they are vertical and then swing them over to one side at right angles to your trunk. Hold for ten seconds and then return to vertical. Repeat to the other side.

Another posture to increase the suppleness of your spine. Start by lying face down with your legs together and your palms on the floor beneath your shoulders. Now raise your head and try to face the ceiling, arching your back and straightening your arms without letting your pelvis leave the floor. Try to hold for ten seconds but do not strain yourself.

Sleep
The average person spends about a third of his life – that is approximately 25 years – asleep, and yet remarkably little is known about what sleep is and why it is necessary.

The assumption is that sleep somehow rests the brain and 'recharges the batteries'. When a feeling of tiredness and sleepiness descends upon us, it is the brain's way of saying that it needs to stop working for a while.

Certainly if anyone is deprived of sleep for more than about three nights, their thoughts and feelings become grossly deranged. Then memory goes, coordination is impaired, they are irritable, unable to concentrate and emotionally unstable. Eventually, they become disorientated and suffer hallucinations and complete mental breakdown.

However, people differ greatly in the amount of sleep they need. Whilst seven to eight hours is average, many people need ten or even eleven hours a night, whilst others can manage apparently quite happily, on only three or four. Generally speaking, the older one gets, the less sleep one seems to need.

Missing a night or two of good sleep does little harm apart from making you touchy and torpid. The brain will make up for the lost sleep just as soon as it gets an uninterrupted chance. This it does, not necessarily by sleeping for longer, but by adjusting the *type* of sleep at different times of the night. The fact is that the type of sleep is more important than the length of time spent sleeping.

There are two basic types of sleep: plain (orthodox) sleep, which will vary in depth, and dream-sleep, sometimes called REM sleep because it is accompanied by rapid eye movements.

It used to be thought that a 'good night's sleep' was one that was unpunctuated by dreams. It now seems that this is not true and that, to be really restful and refreshing, sleep must include a proportion of dream-sleep. In fact, everybody dreams when they sleep; whether they remember them depends on whether they wake during or soon after a bout of dream-sleep.

In laboratory experiments, people have been deprived of their dream-sleep by being woken as soon as the rapid-eye-movements began, although they were allowed a full eight hours of plain-sleep. The result was that they were almost as irritable and uncoordinated as if they had not slept at all. Following such experiments, it is now thought that there is some process, so far unidentified, that is vital for full wakefulness and that it can only occur during dream-sleep, although the dreams themselves are probably not crucial.

From the moment you shut your eyes the electrical rhythms in your brain begin to slow, lulling you first into a state of restfulness and then into a 'twilight' state in which you dip into sleep for a few seconds at a time. These moments of sleep become longer and longer until you drift off completely, slipping deeper and deeper into plain-sleep.

After about 20 minutes you reach a state of profound mental and physical inactivity; your muscles totally relaxed; your heart-rate, blood pressure and temperature at their lowest. This first phase of deep plain-sleep lasts about an hour. Then your brain rhythms start to speed up and your sleep becomes rapidly lighter until you enter a phase of dream-sleep persisting for several minutes.

This cycle is repeated about five times during the night, with periods of dream-sleep occurring about every 90 minutes. As the night wears on, each descent into plain sleep gets shorter and shallower, and each period of dream-sleep longer and lighter.

Altogether the average adult spends about one-fifth of the night in dream-sleep; for children it is twice this amount. Children also have longer bouts of deep sleep, during which the brain secretes a hormone that stimulates growth and repair of tissues.

Insomnia About one person in ten complains of 'insomnia', by which they mean some sort of difficulty getting a good night's sleep. It might be difficulty in getting off to sleep, or sleeping fitfully, or waking too early.

There is a long list of possible causes of insomnia, ranging from a lump in the bed or a snoring spouse, to a chronic anxiety state or severe depression.

Whatever its cause however, if insomnia persists for more than a week or two, a vicious circle is put into motion. Irritability and befuddlement can lead to strained personal relationships, which leads to more trouble in the family or at work; stress builds up, sleeping becomes still more difficult, and so it goes on. As each sleepless night goes by, the brain resets its time-switches, so that it becomes harder to return to a normal sleep pattern. It is at this point that many people seek the advice of their doctor.

Drug-induced versus natural sleep
Although hypno-sedative drugs may induce a state of sleep, the quality is not the same as natural sleep. Whatever type of drug is taken – whether it is a barbiturate, a tranquillizer

Ready for bed. Children need more sleep than adults – especially 'dream-sleep'.

or simply an alcoholic nightcap – it will artificially alter the cycle of brain changes that induce natural sleep. Whilst it is true that these changes have failed (and hence the insomnia), the sleep induced by drugs is a poor substitute since the balance of dream-sleep to plain-sleep is upset. Furthermore, nearly all these drugs have some hangover effect, especially in elderly people, so that the next day is spent less than fully alert, and the following night's sleep pattern will be even more disturbed. The most important factor of all is that many people become psychologically dependent on their sleeping pills, and those on barbiturates may become physically addicted to them, making it extremely difficult to cut down or give them up and return to sleeping naturally.

Sleeping pills can be an invaluable help in times of crisis (such as bereavement) **but should be taken for a few nights only.**

Getting a good night's sleep – naturally It is important to remember that it is natural *not* to sleep well if there is a good reason why. Any upset or problem that preys on the mind can keep you awake. Sometimes a night of fitful sleep occurs for no apparent reason. A certain amount of disturbed sleep, therefore, may be taken in one's stride – without becoming too anxious about it. There are, however, several simple ways of creating the right set of circumstances to help you get a good night's sleep.

1. Do not drink stimulants like coffee, tea or cola within two or three hours of bedtime. A warm bedtime drink on the other hand, can be very relaxing. Warm milk, perhaps with malt or chocolate is ideal. A little alcohol is a harmless and effective nightcap if used occasionally. If you tend to get hungry at night, a biscuit or two with your drink may help, but do not eat spicy or meaty food late at night or your stomach will keep you awake.
2. Soothe mind and body. It helps to really relax before bedtime, by having a long warm bath or listening to soft music. Avoid anything that is likely to cause agitation. The best distractions are those which will provide soothing, gentle pictures to replay in your mind whilst you lie in bed.
3. Make sure your bed and bedroom are as comfortable as possible. It is surprising how uncomfortable it suddenly seems when you cannot sleep. Try to get things as cosy and as restful as possible *before* you go to bed.
4. If there is a nagging problem that runs perpetually through your mind at night, try confronting it by day. This of course is easier said than done, but once confronted the anxiety often melts away.

Programme Your Fitness

Exercise and Health

For many the mere mention of exercise conjures up memories of breathless physical training sessions in the school gym or visions of self-righteous joggers, out in all weathers, pounding the pavement and cursing the commuter traffic. In fact, this is not what exercise is really about.

Exercise does not mean that you have to suffer pain, exhaustion or embarrassment in the name of fitness. Healthy exercise is fun; it can be more exhilarating than any pep-pill; and, most important of all, it protects against the effects of today's sedentary and stressful life.

The human body was built for action. Man is by nature a standing, walking, running, jumping and climbing creature. Primitive man had to hunt for the family meal and his success was entirely dependent on his fleetness of foot, strength of arm, endurance and guile. Primitive woman did not simply stir the soup and nurse the baby – she helped by gathering grain, roots, nuts and fruit and fetching water. In the modern world, however, we run on wheels, we jump in lifts, we climb on escalators and we let our fingers do the walking. Whilst technology takes the drudge out of our lives and gives us more time to relax, our bodies miss their natural exercise and in some respects age more quickly.

Exercise does not exhaust the body – in fact it has the opposite effect and actually stimulates the body's natural maintenance and repair system. If your lifestyle is too sedentary, your joints will become progressively stiffer, your muscles will become more and more flabby and your arteries will become silted up with fatty deposits, so that your heart is more prone to disease. Regular exercise – even if it is only moderately vigorous – can help to prevent these problems; it speeds up the body's metabolic rate, thus reducing any tendency to put on weight. At the same time, mood-lifting brain hormones are secreted. The overall result is that one looks better, feels better and stays 'younger'.

Exercise and weight

There is no doubt that regular moderate exercise helps obese people to slim. Although dieting is the single most effective means of weight reduction in most cases, some obese people find that even a fairly strict diet is only partly successful. Such people probably have a rather lower general metabolic rate – that is, they burn up their energy intake rather more slowly – and therefore tend to deposit rather more body fat. Bouts of physical activity burn up energy faster. Slimmers may be disappointed to discover that they would have to jog for three-quarters of an hour to work off the calories in a modest 60 g ($2\frac{1}{2}$ oz) piece of cheese or two glasses of white wine, but if exercise is taken *vigorously and frequently* enough, the effect lasts much longer as the general metabolic rate is increased. This means that calories are burned up a little faster *all the time,* even when relaxing or sleeping.

Exercise and the heart

There is mounting evidence that *regular* moderate exercise protects against coronary heart disease. A recent survey of civil servants in sedentary jobs found that those who took moderately vigorous exercise in their leisure time (at least 20 minutes three times a week) had far fewer heart attacks than their inactive colleagues. Regular exercise also alters the balance of fatty substances in the bloodstream, slows the resting pulse-rate and lowers the resting blood-pressure. At the same time the heart muscle itself is strengthened and beats more regularly.

Exercise and young people

Children seldom go short of exercise. Even quiet, unadventurous, overweight or short-sighted children almost certainly get a healthy helping of activity forced on them by their more energetic playmates or at school. Adolescents, school leavers and young adults, however, often take progressively less and less interest in games and sports, except perhaps as a spectator. Parents can help by encouraging children to enjoy exercise from an early age and persuading them to join in family sports and games. Exercise need not be competitive and should always be fun.

What is fitness?

Physical fitness may be defined as being able to **cope comfortably** with the various physical demands of everyday life, including those occasions when a little extra, or a little longer, effort is required. Obviously a young man should be able to achieve a considerably higher level of physical capability than an elderly lady, but nevertheless they can both be adequately **fit** for their ages and lifestyles.

There is also another aspect to fitness – that of **long term protection.** The fact that exercise can help to protect against chronic disease and disability, makes it important to maintain a certain degree of physical capability for as long as possible.

There are three fundamental components of physical fitness – *stamina, suppleness* and *strength,* and 'Fitness' means paying sufficient attention to all three.

Stamina

This is staying power or 'aerobic endurance'; the ability to keep going without collapsing at the knees and running short of breath. It depends on the efficiency of the body's muscles and circulation, including its most important 'muscle' – the heart. Those who possess a fair measure of stamina, have a slower, more powerful heartbeat; they can cope more easily with greater exertion for a longer period of time, and their chances of avoiding a heart attack are improved.

Stamina is brought about by the ability of the heart and skeletal muscles to take up vital oxygen and release waste products that cause fatigue. These aspects can be vastly improved by rhythmic, dynamic contraction of large groups of muscles against constant resistance – the result is known as the 'aerobic training effect'. So brisk walking, jogging, skipping, heavy digging, cycling or swimming are all good stamina-building exercises providing they are done vigorously enough, for long enough and frequently enough to achieve the training effect. A suitable stamina-building programme would consist of any sport or activity with a stamina score of two or more on the Fitness Factor Chart, performed sufficiently vigorously to produce moderate breathlessness, continued for at least 20 minutes at a time and repeated at least twice a week.

Suppleness

This is flexibility (and hence mobility) and it is a particularly important fitness factor for middle-aged and elderly people who are increasingly prone to stiffness, sprains and strains. When joints become 'stiff' through disuse or increasing age, the ligaments, muscles and tendons shorten and become weaker. The net result is that the range of movement of the joint is reduced, and if it is excessively bent or straightened – perhaps by an awkward fall – the ligaments could be sprained and the muscles or tendons pulled.

By performing suitable suppleness exercises (see page 54) it is possible to develop maximum range of movement of the neck, back and limbs, thereby improving physical agility and reducing the risk of pains from muscle, tendon and ligament injury.

Suppleness exercises, which need only take a few minutes, are best performed daily. Other sports and activities which improve suppleness are shown as having a suppleness score of two or more on the chart (right).

Strength

This is muscle power; the ability to exert a sustained force for a limited length of time. Strength is an important fitness factor at all ages. In youth it provides the power for vigorous work and play. In middle-age it is needed in reserve for unexpectedly heavy jobs such as lifting and shifting, while the elderly need to maximize their strength to help them go about their daily activities and maintain their independence.

Strength is improved by regular exercises consisting of muscle contraction against resistance. These exercises may be either **isometric** – in which the resistance is not allowed to give way and the muscle thus contracts without actually shortening (for example, weightlifting) – or **dynamic** (isotonic), in which the resistance gives way as the muscle contracts and shortens (for example, cycling). Both types of exercise increase strength and muscle bulk, although there is some evidence that isometric exercises are more effective as body builders. Against that is the fact that isometrics cause peaks of blood pressure which could be dangerous for people over the age of 35 whose arteries are less resilient. Dynamic strength exercises are generally safer for such people.

Sports and activities which help to improve strength are those with a strength score of two or more on the chart below.

The chart below gives rough estimates of how effective various activities are for developing each of the three fitness factors: stamina, suppleness and strength.

FITNESS-FACTOR CHART

	Stamina	Suppleness	Strength
Badminton	••	•••	••
Climbing Stairs	•••	•	••
Cycling (hard)	••••	••	•••
Dancing (disco)	•••	••••	•
Digging (garden)	•••	••	••••
Football	•••	•••	•••
Golf	•	••	•
Gymnastics	••	••••	•••
Hill Walking	•••	•	••
Housework (moderate)	•	••	•
Jogging	••••	••	••
Squash	•••	•••	••
Swimming (hard)	••••	••••	••••
Tennis	••	•••	••
Walking (briskly)	••	•	•
Yoga	•	•••	•

• Negligible effect ••• Very useful effect
•• Useful effect •••• Excellent effect

How fit are you?

The best tests of overall fitness are those that measure *stamina*. Below are four very simple graduated tests. Test one should be well within most people's capability, except perhaps the very unfit, frail or elderly. Tests two, three and four are progressively more demanding and each one should not be attempted until the previous test can be achieved comfortably. These tests will determine your 'Fitness Grade', which you can use as a guide to the Fitness Training Programme. The yardstick used in these tests is the degree of *breathlessness*. You should not be more than mildly breathless, so that you could still hold a conversation without having to break sentences to breathe.

An alternative, and more precise yardstick is the *pulse-rate*. The normal pulse-rate in a healthy young adult at rest averages 72 to 76 beats per minute for men and 75 to 80 for women; but the rate can vary from 50 to 100 according to fitness. The fitter you are, the lower your pulse rate.

Exercise increases the pulse rate, again according to fitness. The pulse rate of a reasonably fit person who spends a few minutes jogging will increase by about ten beats a minute, whereas in an unfit person, the rate could double.

The Pulse-rate Test (right) measures your Fitness Grade and also provides you with a 'Pulse-rate Handicap' which you can use to calculate your 'target' pulse-rate for stamina-building. This is the rate you should aim for in all your stamina building activities. If your pulse-rate exceeds this figure, stop and rest until it falls below it again.

Sensible precautions

Most people do not need a medical check-up before starting an exercise programme. But everyone must be sensible about the programme they attempt. You must choose the activities that are appropriate – begin them very gently and increase the effort very gradually, to gain the benefits without putting a strain on yourself.

However, it would be wise to consult your doctor if you are receiving regular medication for a known medical condition; you are recovering from a recent illness or operation; you have (or have had) pains in the head, neck, chest, back or limbs when you exert yourself; or you are worried that regular exercise may affect some other aspect of your health. In particular, if you have had a coronary, high blood pressure, diabetes or arthritis, it is best to seek your doctor's advice before planning an exercise schedule.

Graduated Stamina Tests

Test One Walk up and down a flight of 15 steps fairly briskly, *three* times. (Stop before this if you feel at all uncomfortable.) If you are more than mildly breathless, you are very unfit (Fitness Grade 1) and should not attempt any further tests. Check the Sensible Precautions opposite before undertaking vigorous activity, including the Fitness Training Programme. If you wish to start the Programme begin very gently at Grade 1.

Test Two Run on the spot, picking your feet up 20 cm (8 in) off the floor. Continue for three minutes then stop. (Stop before if you feel at all uncomfortable.) If you are more than mildly breathless, you are fairly unfit (Fitness Grade 2) and should not attempt any further tests. If you wish to follow the Fitness Training Programme, start at Grade 2.

Test Three Using either the *second* step on the stairs (or a firm bench or strong chair), step up and down briskly – left leg up, right leg up, left leg down, right leg down – at the rate of two complete steps every five seconds. Continue for two minutes if you are aged 45 or over, or three if aged under 45. (Stop before if you feel at all uncomfortable.) If you are anything more than mildly breathless you are at best only partly fit (Fitness Grade 3) and should not attempt any further tests. If you wish to follow the Fitness Training Programme, start at grade 3.

Test Four Do not attempt this unless you found Test Three comfortable and have taken heed of the Sensible Precautions (opposite). Jog gently and easily for 1·6 km (1 mile). (Stop before if you feel at all uncomfortable.) Pace it so that you complete the distance in roughly the following times according to age and sex:

Age	Men	Women
Under 45	10 minutes	12 minutes
45 to 49	11 minutes	13 minutes
50 to 54	12 minutes	14 minutes
55 to 59	13 minutes	15 minutes
60 to 64	14 minutes	16 minutes

If you are only mildly breathless you are fairly fit (Fitness Grade 4). If you are more than mildly breathless, you are Fitness Grade 3. In either case start the Fitness Training Programme at the appropriate Grade.

The Pulse Rate Test
Using the first step of the stairs, or any other step of 20 cm (8 in), step up and down briskly for three minutes alternating your leading foot. Aim at a rate of two complete steps every five seconds. (If you feel uncomfortable at any stage stop immediately.) Rest for exactly one minute and then take your pulse (see right).

Pulse Rate Men	Pulse Rate Women	Fitness Handicap	Training Grade
under 80	under 85	10	4
80 to 89	85 to 94	20	3
90 to 99	95 to 109	30	2
100 plus	110 plus	40	1

Start the Progressive Training Programme at the Grade indicated.

If you wish to follow the Fitness Training Programme, start at the Grade indicated.

To calculate your 'target' pulse-rate for stamina-building, subtract your age from 200, and then subtract your Pulse-Rate Handicap. The resulting figure is your 'target' pulse-rate in beats per minute. Do not exceed this rate when exercising.

Getting fit
The most important thing about getting fit is keeping fit – it's not much good if it's just a nine-day wonder – and the most important thing about keeping fit is to choose activities you *enjoy*. The Fitness-Factor Chart on page 51 gives the stamina, suppleness and strength scores of some of the most popular activities. Choose activities that are best for the Fitness-Factors most important to you, but always begin each activity with a simple warm-up routine of suppleness exercises as shown on page 54. Note that the activities that are best for stamina (and hence overall fitness) consist of dynamic exercise of large muscle groups – such as brisk walking, jogging, cycling, swimming or rowing.

For those who prefer specific exercises, a Fitness Training Programme is shown on page 56.

Whatever form of exercise you choose to follow, always start **gently** and build up the routine **gradually.** Never attempt vigorous competitive games until you have reached a good level of fitness.

It is important that you enjoy your activities because for full benefit, exercise should be taken regularly, for at least 20 minutes, three times a week. It will take at least two to three weeks before you notice any real physical benefit, although you might feel elated long before then.

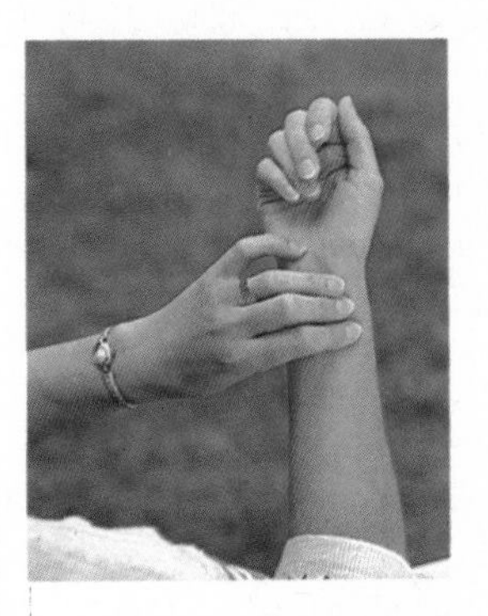

To take your pulse, place a watch or clock (with a second hand) in a spot where you can see it. Turn one of your hands palm upwards and place the first three fingers of the other hand lightly on to the wrist about 2·5–5 cm (1–2 in) up the arm from the heel of the thumb. The pulse can be felt about half-way between the tendon and the arm-bone. Count the number of beats in fifteen seconds and multiply by four to give the pulse-rate per minute.

Suppleness Exercises for Warming-Up

Before any vigorous activity, it is important to spend a few minutes limbering up with some simple bending and stretching exercises. These not only help to loosen the joints and improve their range of movement, but also tone up the major muscle groups, preparing them for action. The exercises should preferably be performed daily, and a good time to do them is first thing in the morning as they are an excellent way of waking up.

Here are six movements to do in an easy unhurried manner, gently stretching (not bouncing) each action to its fullest **comfortable** range without forcing it, breathing easily as you stretch. They are **not** physical jerks. Repeat each exercise six times.

1. Deep breathing
Stand comfortably with your feet together, arms by your sides. Breathe steadily out as far as you can, using your tummy muscles by pulling them in to push out the last little puff of air. Then breathe in really deeply, letting your ribcage expand. This exercise gets fresh air to the corners of your lungs.

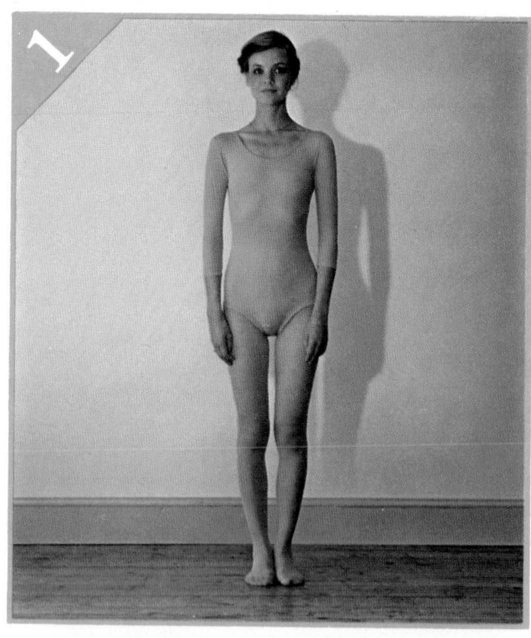

2. Head rolling
Stand comfortably with your feet together, arms by your sides. Tip your head back as far as is comfortable and look up at the ceiling. Roll your head round slowly to face the right, then downwards, then towards the left and finally up at the ceiling again. Repeat in the other direction. Do not worry if a somewhat 'gritty' sound comes from your neck.

3. Arm swinging
Stand with your feet comfortably apart and hold both arms straight out in front of you, fingertips touching. Raise them straight above your head, brushing your ears, and then down to the sides pushing each arm backwards as you go.

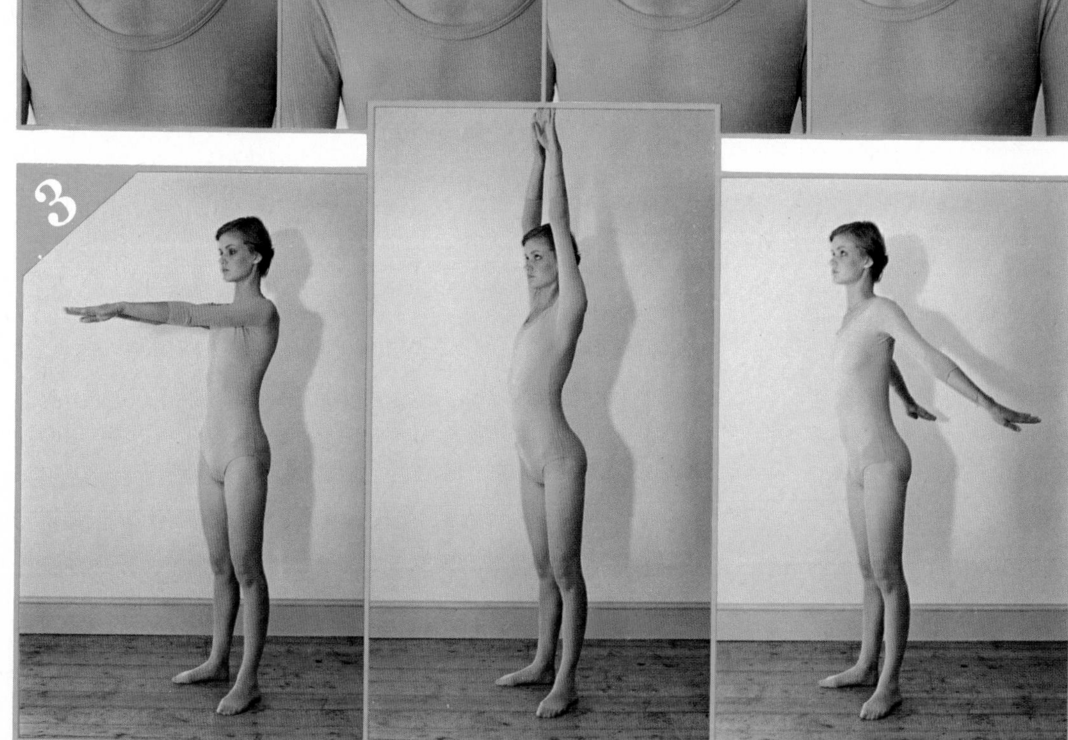

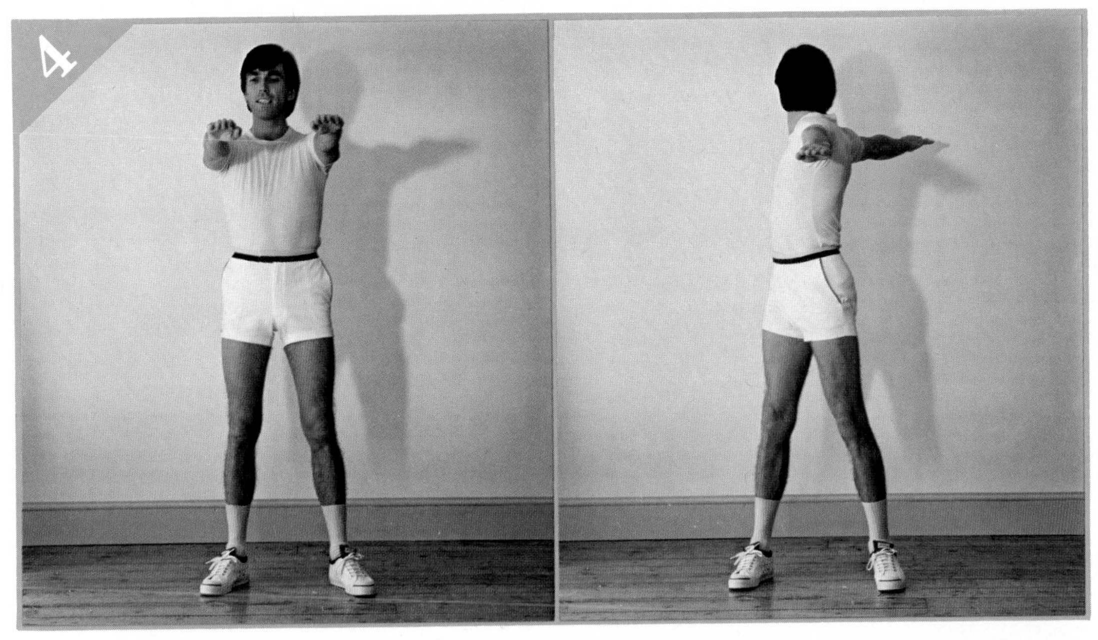

4. Trunk twisting
Stand with your feet apart, arms straight out in front of you. Fix your eyes on your right hand and swing your right arm round to the right as far as it will comfortably go, keeping it straight. Return it to the front and repeat with the left arm, watching the left hand as it swings.

5. Side bending
Still with your feet apart, put your hands down to your sides and lean your head and trunk to the right, sliding your hand further down the side of your leg. Return to the vertical and repeat to the left.

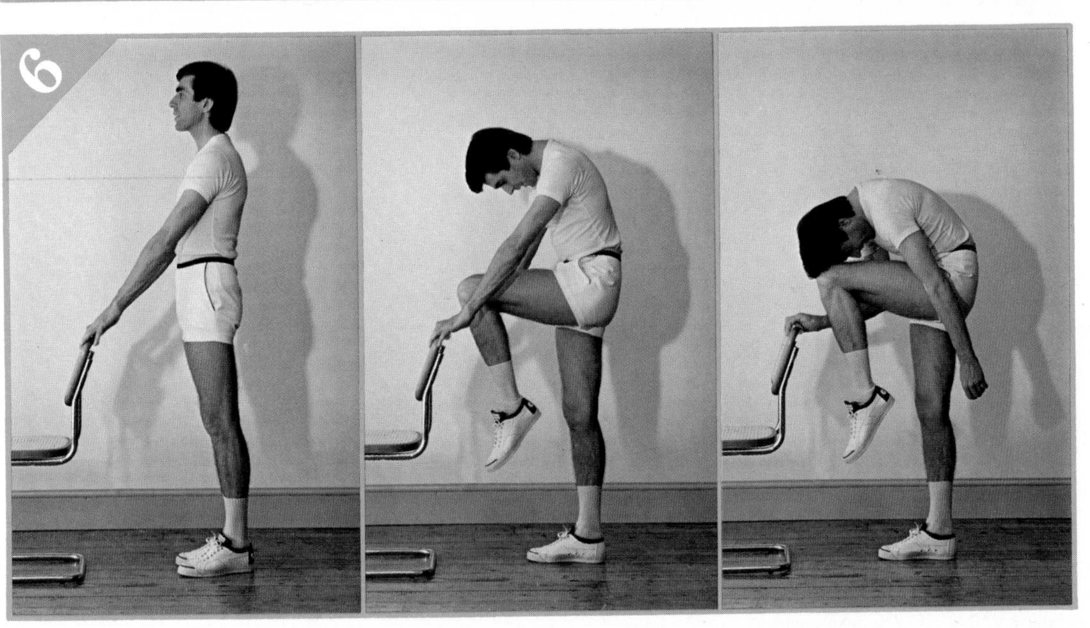

6. Spine, hip and knee flexing
Stand, feet together (if necessary, behind a sturdy chair with your hands resting on the back). Now slowly raise one knee and at the same time bend your head and trunk forward. Try to touch your knee on your forehead or at least get it as close as is comfortable. Repeat with the other knee.

Fitness Training Programme

This is a simple all-purpose training programme suitable for adults or older children of either sex, from the already fit to the very unfit (but see Sensible Precautions, page 52).

The Programme is divided into three basic *strength exercises* (sit-ups, press-ups and star-jumps) and a *stamina-building schedule* based on jogging. Running on the spot, skipping, swimming or cycling can be substituted for jogging as long as the guidelines about breathlessness or pulse-rates are followed.

You should aim at a minimum of three training sessions a week, each lasting at least 30 minutes. Start by spending two or three minutes warming up with the suppleness exercises on page 54 followed by 7 or 8 minutes of the strength exercises and a final 20 minutes of stamina-building.

Choose the correct exercises for your Fitness Grade and do not move up a grade until you can manage each exercise comfortably.

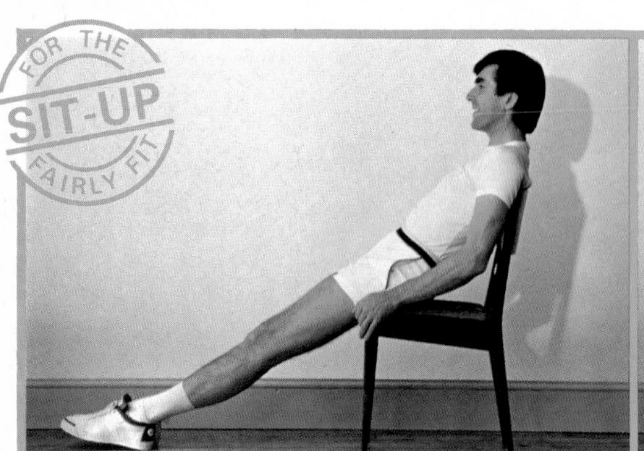

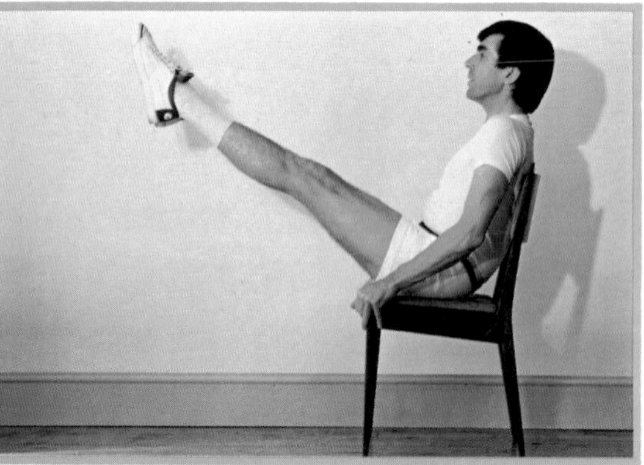

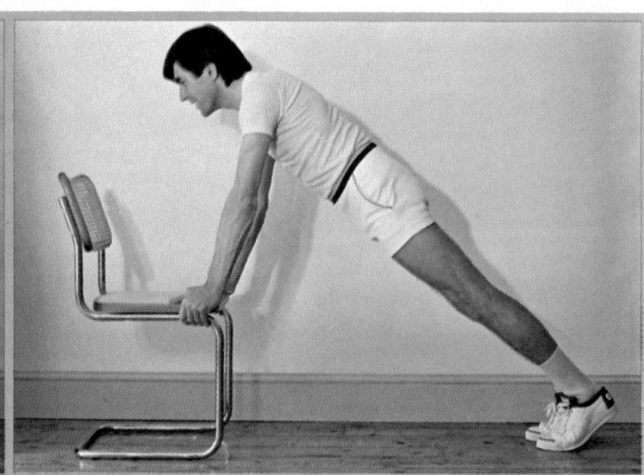

Sit-up for the fairly fit. For Fitness Grades 1 and 2. Lean back on a chair with legs straight in front. Lift legs slowly to 45° above horizontal. Hold 10 seconds, then relax.

Sit-up for the very fit. For Fitness Grades 3 and 4. Lie flat on your back with feet on a chair and hands behind head. Sit up slowly to vertical. Hold 10 seconds, then relax.

Press-up for the fairly fit. For Fitness Grades 1 and 2. Use a firm, steady chair. Keeping body straight, raise and lower yourself slowly with your arms.

Press-up for the very fit. For Fitness Grades 3 and 4. Hands on floor under shoulders. Body straight. Raise and lower yourself slowly with your arms.

Star-jump for the fairly fit. For Fitness Grades 1 and 2. Squat with hands on hips. Straighten slowly to stand on toes. Return slowly to squat.

Star-jump for the very fit. For Fitness Grades 3 and 4. Squat with hands on hips. Straighten quickly to 'star-jump' into the air. Land back in squat position.

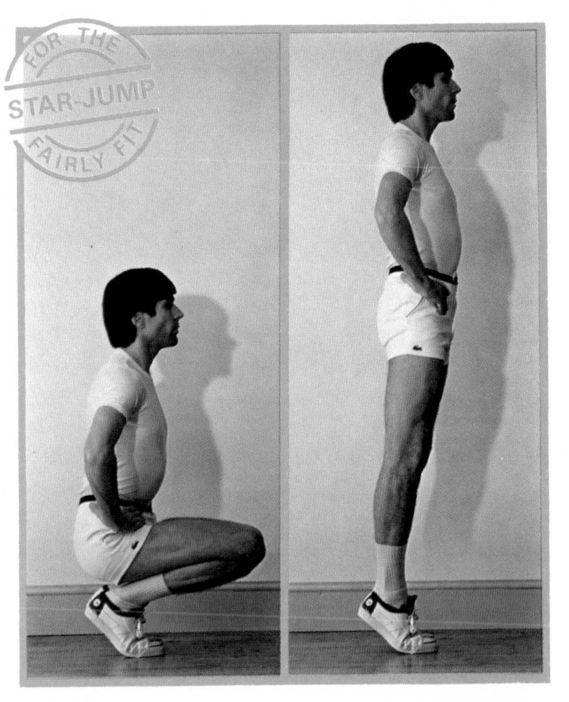

JOGGING PLAN A

For over 35-year-olds or people who are rather out of condition (i.e. Fitness Grades 1 and 2)

Week 1	Take every opportunity to walk in this first week. Walk upstairs instead of using the lift. Walk the last part of the bus journey. Try to build up to at least half-an-hour's brisk walking each day.
Week 2	Find time for three or more half-hour exercise sessions a week. Begin each session with suppleness and strength exercises. Then walk briskly for 10 minutes, followed by 5 minutes of alternate jogging and walking (10 seconds of jogging, then 10 seconds' walking, and so on). Finish with another 5 minutes' walking.
Week 3	Walk briskly for 5 minutes. Then 5 minutes of alternate jogging and walking in 30-second bursts of each. Then walk for 2 minutes. Then alternate jogging/walking as before for another 5 minutes. Finish with 5 minutes' walking.
Week 4	Walk briskly for 2 minutes. Then alternate jogging/walking in one-minute bursts of each for 5 minutes. Then walk for 2 minutes. Then another 5 minutes of jogging/walking as before. Finish with 5 minutes' walking.
Week 5	Walk briskly for 2 minutes. Then alternate jogging/walking in one-minute bursts for 15 minutes. Finish with a 2-minute walk.
Week 6	Walk briskly for 1 minute. Jog for 2 minutes. Walk 1 minute. Jog 2 minutes. Repeat this alternately for the full 20 minutes finishing with a one-minute walk.
Week 7 onwards	Begin by walking briskly for 1 minute. Then jog with walking breaks every few minutes. Week by week have fewer and shorter walking breaks until you are jogging comfortably for the whole 20-minute session.

JOGGING PLAN B

For under 35-year-olds or people who are already fairly fit (i.e. Fitness Grades 3 and 4).

Week 1	Find time for three or more half-hour exercise sessions a week. Begin each session with suppleness and strength exercises. Then walk briskly for 5 minutes. Follow this with alternate jogging and walking, in 30-second bursts of each, for a total of 10 minutes. Finish by walking for 5 minutes.
Week 2	Walk briskly for 2 minutes. Then alternate jogging/walking, in one-minute bursts of each, for a total of 15 minutes. Finish with a 2-minute walk.
Week 3	Walk briskly for 1 minute. Then jog for 2 minutes. Repeat this walking 1 minute, jogging 2 minutes for the whole 20-minute session finishing with a 1-minute walk.
Week 4 onwards	Begin by walking briskly for 1 minute. Then jog with walking breaks every few minutes. Week by week have fewer and shorter walking breaks until eventually you are jogging comfortably for the whole 20-minute session.

Pedalling for Pleasure

Cycling is not only an excellent stamina-builder, it also has the advantages of getting you from place to place. To be a really effective exercise you need to exert yourself sufficiently to become mildly breathless, preferably for at least 20 minutes, three times a week.

Cycling has another important advantage over other stamina-exercises like walking and jogging; you do not have to take your weight on your feet. This means it is superb exercise for people with hip, knee or foot trouble and allows them to build up stamina without the pain of weight-bearing.

A few don'ts

Don't cycle at night without efficient lights. Wear light-coloured or reflective clothing.

Don't let your cycle fall into disrepair. In particular, check your brakes regularly.

Don't change lanes or turn without first glancing behind to make sure it is safe and giving a clear hand signal.

Don't cycle in icy conditions.

Don't cycle in fog.

Swimming

Swimming is just about the best all-round form of exercise and is ideal for developing all three Fitness Factors. Apart from that, the sensual delight of being caressed by the water is extremely relaxing and refreshing.

To get the full benefit from swimming, each session should include a variety of different strokes, so that different groups of muscles and joints are exercised. For example, whilst the breaststroke is best for hips and knees, the backstroke or crawl are better for shoulders and trunk. As you swim, concentrate on a good stretch, streamlined body position, smooth steady stroke and deep breaths in time with the action.

Swimming is extremely beneficial for those who are overweight or have arthritis, back trouble or muscle weakness. Because the body is supported by the water, the joints can be worked without the discomfort of weight-bearing. It is also an all-weather, all-year round activity as most pools are heated and indoors.

Try to spend at least 20 minutes, three times a week in the pool, building up the activity slowly, without tiring yourself or getting more than mildly breathless.

A few don'ts

Don't swim within two hours of a heavy meal.

Don't let yourself get too cold, or you may get cramp.

Don't swim where there are dangerous currents or tides.

Jogging

Jogging is running free and easy at a pace that makes you no more than mildly breathless. This should be a comfortable 'trot'; there is no hurry, no competition, and no record to break.

The joy of jogging is that it is one of the most natural and effective ways of exercising the heart and lungs, and building up stamina. The steady repetitive rhythm of jogging has a remarkably relaxing and euphoric effect easing away mental and physical stress and lifting depression. It can be enjoyed by virtually anyone – young or old; anytime, anywhere; alone or with a friend. Indeed it is an activity the whole family can do together.

As with any stamina exercise, it is vital to start very *gently* and build up the effort very *gradually*, week-by-week (see page 57). This gives the muscles, heart and circulation time to adapt and develop in response to the increased demand.

Building up and maintaining stamina requires about 20 minutes of sustained effort, three times a week. Always start each session with a suppleness warm-up (page 54). If you feel at all uncomfortable whilst jogging – stop. You should never be more than mildly breathless, and your pulse-rate should not rise above your target rate for stamina-building (page 53).

A few don'ts

Don't jog within two hours of your last meal.
Don't jog if you feel tired, weak or washed out.
Don't jog if you have a cold or feel as if you are starting one.
Don't jog in the fog.

Mainly for Women

Because of their role in human reproduction, women face a number of special health problems that men are spared, and indeed are largely unaware of.

Cancer Checks

Many women turn a blind eye to the risk of cancer of the breast, either refusing to accept that it could happen to them or reckoning that if there is something wrong it will show itself up sooner or later. These are both understandable reactions to the horrible prospect of having to lose a breast, but there are two important reasons why it is actually less worrying in the long run to come to terms with the risk and to examine your breasts regularly for signs of abnormality.

Firstly, the great majority of breast abnormalities are caused by such simple, harmless or easily treated conditions as blocked milk-ducts, periodic breast lumpiness (adenosis), benign tumours and abscess scars. Secondly, in the few cases that do turn out to be cancer, the sooner it is treated the better the chance of a complete cure before it starts to spread.

How to examine your breasts

Examine your breasts every month; ideally just after the menstrual period if you are still having periods. At this time, periodic breast lumpiness is at a minimum. You are checking for the presence of anything new or different from your usual breast appearance or consistency, but bear in mind that your breasts are normally likely to be of slightly unequal shape and size, and that the normal consistency is generally vaguely lumpy.

If you think you may have found something unusual make an appointment to see your doctor. It is never a waste of a doctor's time to give an opinion on any suspicious change in a woman's breasts.

Cervix – The Smear Test

Although cancer of the cervix (the neck of the womb) is fairly rare, it is nevertheless the second most common cancer affecting women – the most common being cancer of the breast. Fortunately, it can be detected at the pre-cancerous stage and all traces removed by a simple operation under local anaesthetic before cancer develops.

The detection test is the cervical 'smear', performed as a routine when having a family planning, gynaecological or ante-natal examination. A small wooden spatula is simply wiped around the mouth of the womb to collect some surface cells and secretions. This smear is then examined under a microscope.

The progression from pre-cancerous to cancer itself takes place over a period of years and so it is not necessary to have smears performed more often than about once every three years. If your GP does not perform cervical smears, the receptionist will tell you where you can have the test done.

Cystitis

This is a very common, but nonetheless troublesome, complaint amongst women. It produces a feeling of constantly needing to pass water, but when an attempt is made to do so it is accompanied by a burning discomfort and very little urine. The urine may be cloudy, smoky or bloodstained. These symptoms are usually due to an inflammation of the sensitive bladder lining and its equally sensitive outlet pipe, the urethra, caused either by micro-organisms ascending from the outer vagina, or by over-vigorous intercourse which may bruise the urethra.

Occasionally the infection ascends beyond the bladder and up to the kidneys. This is a much more serious situation and is a particular problem in young girls whose urinary systems are still growing. Because of this danger, it is always important to seek medical advice if symptoms persist for more than 24 hours.

Self-help for a cystitis attack

1. Urination helps to flush out germs, so keep drinking plenty of fluids – 300 ml (about ½ pint) every 20 minutes for the first three hours, and every hour thereafter (until one hour before bedtime).
2. Take bicarbonate of soda – one teaspoon in water every hour for the first three hours.
3. Keep warm – a hot water bottle on your tummy may bring some relief.
4. A mild pain killer such as paracetamol or soluble aspirin may also be helpful.

Prevention

If you suffer from recurrent cystitis, try the following simple preventive measures:

1. Drink about 2 litres (5 pints) of bland fluid a day – not all tea or coffee!
2 Always wipe 'down below' from **front to back** to avoid infection from the anus.
3. Wash these parts with a separate flannel and do not use strong soaps, detergents or antiseptics – just plain water.
4. If attacks are related to intercourse, make sure you and your partner wash thoroughly with plain water beforehand. If necessary use a gel lubricant to prevent soreness and bruis-

Look First

1. Undressed to the waist, sit or stand in front of a mirror, arms comfortably by your sides. Make sure you are in a good light. Look for any change in appearance; any puckering or dimpling of the skin; any change in the outline; any discharge or bleeding from the nipple.
2. Raise your arms above your head. Turn from side to side and look again for changes since last month.
3. Put your hands on your hips and push them inwards, tightening your chest muscles and looking for puckering or dimples.
Lift up each breast and look at the undersides.

Then Feel

4. Lie down on a bed, put a folded towel under one shoulder and raise the arm putting it behind your head, thus stretching your breast on that side.
With the other hand gently feel each imaginary quarter of the breast, using the flat of the hand, not the tips of the fingers.
Start with the upper inner quarter, feeling from the edge of the breast towards the nipple.
5. Next, feel the lower inner quarter, again working towards the nipple.
6. Now bring your arm to your side and feel the lower outer quarter.
7. Finally, feel the upper outer quarter, which is the commonest place for breast lumps. There is a little extension of breast tissue outwards from this quarter to the armpit. Feel this carefully and feel in the armpit itself for lumps.
Repeat from step 4 to examine the other breast.

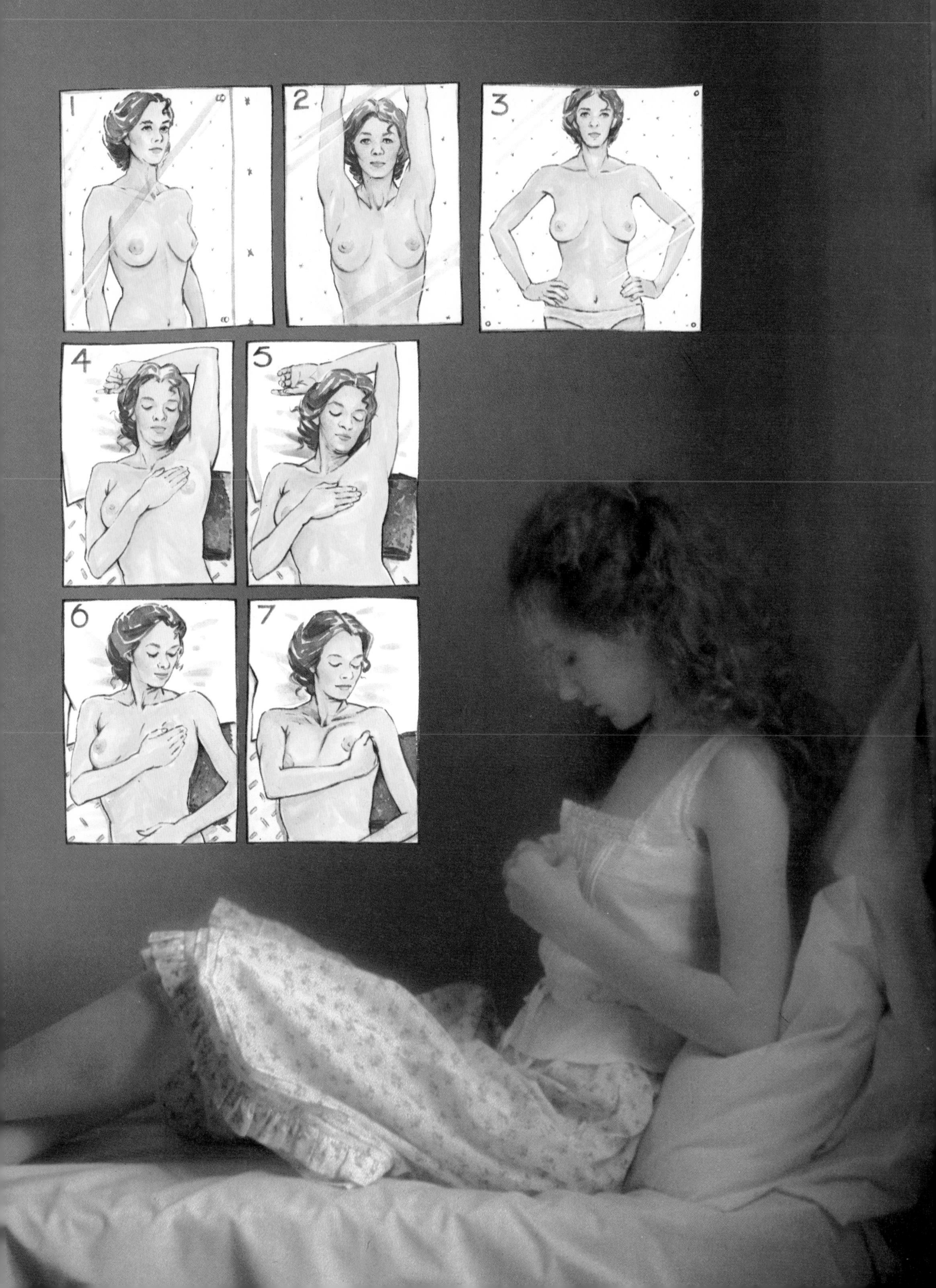
1
2
3
4
5
6
7

ing on intercourse. Empty your bladder within about 15 minutes of finishing.

5. If there is a persistent discharge which is different in any way from usual, or if your partner has urethral discomfort or discharge, then you (or he) should seek the advice of your doctor, or make a telephone appointment with the Department of Genitourinary Medicine (Special Clinic) at your local district hospital. This simple check-up is well worthwhile **whether or not** you think it is likely to be a sexually-transmitted infection.

Period Problems

By far the two commonest problems associated with the menstrual cycle are premenstrual tension and period pains (dysmenorrhoea). These two complaints severely incapacitate millions of women each month.

Both conditions seem to be caused by disturbances of the delicate balance of hormones which control the monthly production of the egg and preparation of the womb lining, and both respond in different ways to hormone treatment. However, there are several practical ways in which a woman can help herself.

Premenstrual Syndrome (PMS)

PMS causes mental and physical symptoms in the second half of the menstrual cycle. The trouble can last anything from a day or two to a week or two before the period and usually has the same duration each month. The physical symptoms might include abdominal swelling and a bloated feeling, breast swelling and discomfort, severe headaches, facial acne and an aching back and limbs. The mental symptoms might include irritability, anxiety, irrational behaviour, depression, loss of concentration and loss of libido or sex drive.

Obviously such problems can cause considerable family upsets, particularly when husband and children do not fully understand the reason for them.

Incidentally, PMS is not related to period pains; nor is it cured by having a baby – indeed it may be worsened.

The first thing is to try to arrange your life as much as possible so that you can cope more easily during the critical days. Husbands, fathers, children, friends and work-mates can help by understanding the problem and offering unobtrusive assistance.

Your doctor can also help in several ways. He might consider prescribing a diuretic which reduces fluid retention and relieves bloatedness and irritability in milder cases. Alternatively, he might prescribe hormone treatment, consisting of any of several drugs which mimic the action of the female hormone progesterone, perhaps as part of a contraceptive pill. Another promising line of treatment is Vitamin B6 (pyridoxine), which also seems to help if the course is started before the symptoms appear.

Period Pains

These can be quite severe cramps in the sides, spreading round to the lower belly and perhaps the inner thighs. They tend to be at their worst during the late teens and early twenties. Then they improve slowly and are usually rapidly improved by having a baby.

Taking soluble aspirin or paracetamol at the first twinge of pain, having a stiff drink, sitting in a warm bath, or lying down with a hot water bottle, are all traditional ways of providing relief. In severe cases, the doctor may prescribe a drug which soothes the painful contractions of the womb, or, if appropriate, hormone treatment. Older women with period pains of recent onset may need special tests to find the cause.

Rubella vaccination

Rubella (German measles) is a mild illness, but it is very dangerous for unborn babies. If a woman catches the disease during early pregnancy, there is a high risk that her baby will be miscarried or stillborn, or, if alive, will suffer physical or mental handicaps, including possibly deafness, blindness, heart defects and mental retardation.

It is therefore extremely important for every woman or girl of childbearing age to be immune to rubella. Those who have never had the disease can have a simple vaccination, which confers almost 100 percent protection. Those who have had the disease will already be immune, unless they suffered an exceptionally mild attack which failed to stimulate immunity. This can be checked by a simple blood test.

Rubella vaccination is now offered to schoolgirls aged 10 to 13, regardless of whether they have had the disease. However, many women of child-bearing age are either too old to have had these school vaccinations, or missed them at the time. If this applies to you (or your daughter), or if you are in any doubt – even if you think you may have had the disease itself – ask your doctor for the blood test and, if it shows you have no immunity, have the vaccination. But remember you must then wait at least **three months** before becoming pregnant.

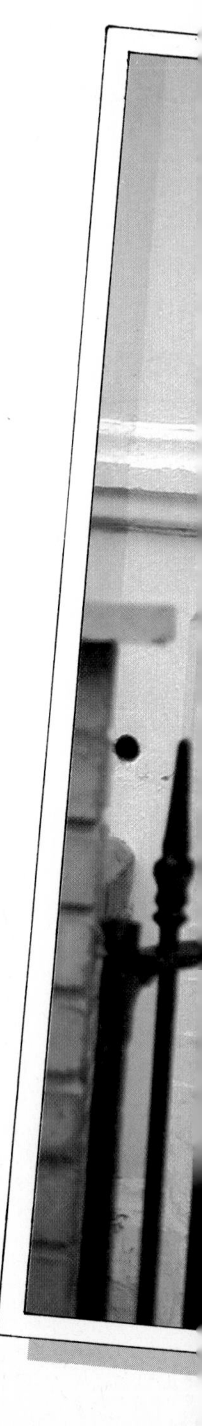

Once the family are older, there is more time for pursuing fresh interests outside the home.

The Menopause

'The Change of Life' marks the end of a woman's reproductive potential, thus ending a chapter of her life. For three out of every four women, it is also a time of emotional and physical turmoil.

Sometime between her early forties and late fifties, a woman's periods become increasingly irregular and then stop altogether. They may even stop quite suddenly. The symptoms that accompany this are collectively called the 'menopausal syndrome'. They are all caused by the widespread effects of the hormonal changes that trigger the menopause.

The symptoms can range from relatively simple nuisances such as tiredness, irritability, headaches, dizzy spells, loss of concentration, pins and needles, constipation and flatulence, to more troublesome problems such as depression, insomnia, hot flushes, vaginal dryness, itchy skin and palpitations.

Depression: Depression often accompanies the menopause. It is depression in the true sense of the word – a 'black cloud' descends on the sufferer, she becomes slow, lethargic and weepy and has no will or energy to resist such feelings. Once the depression sets in, it is difficult for the sufferer to do much about it. This is where the family are important in keeping her stimulated and encouraging, even forcing, her to take an interest in life outside as well as in herself. If depression becomes really severe, medical help must be sought.

Hot flushes These are often the worst symptom, and may be accompanied by 'drenches' or sudden very heavy sweats, especially at night. They can be prevented to some extent by avoiding situations which tend to make the sufferer flush – hot drinks, alcohol, spicy food or even embarrassment. If the flushes persist for more than a month or so, and are interfering with the sufferer's day-to-day existence, she should see her doctor.

Vaginal dryness This is a distressing symptom which many women interpret to mean the end of their sex life. Far from it; with regular use of a lubricant jelly the problem diminishes and with an oestrogen cream or pessary, it can be temporarily reversed.

Incidentally, contraception should be continued for a year after the last period if the change occurs under the age of 50 or for six months if it occurs over this age.

HRT – Hormone Replacement Therapy
Most of the symptoms of the menopause are caused by a lack of oestrogen, and in recent years oestrogen therapy – HRT – has been used to relieve hot flushes, night drenches, and vaginal dryness. It may also be beneficial in some of the other menopausal symptoms.

However, there are still doubts about the long-term safety of HRT. Some specialists claim that it increases the risk of cancer of the uterus, whereas others maintain that this is not a danger if low doses are prescribed. New forms of HRT, which include the hormone progestogen, may prove to be safer, but if it is a matter that concerns you, you should discuss the pros and cons thoroughly with your doctor.

FAMILY PLANNING

Every woman has the right to plan her family by controlling conception so that she has babies when – and only when – she wants them and is in a position to look after them. There is now a wide range of contraceptive measures available to all women of child-bearing age. Here is a brief guide to the most widely used methods. All are safer than the risks involved in having a baby or an abortion.

Where to obtain advice and supplies
Your GP will give advice and may be prepared to prescribe the pill, but may not be trained to fit IUDs or caps. You may register with a GP, other than your own, specifically for contraceptive care.
An alternative is to go directly to your local Family Planning Clinic (run by the local health authority). You do not have to see your GP first. All records are confidential and all advice and prescriptions are on the NHS. People of both sexes, all ages, married or single are welcome at family planning clinics.
For further details and advice on any aspect of family planning, fertility or infertility write or telephone the Family Planning Information Service.

What it is	How it works	How reliable	How convenient	Hazards	Other comments
COMBINED PILL					
A pill taken daily for 21 days then stopped for 7 days to bring on a period. Consists of a synthetic oestrogen combined with a progestogen (similar to the natural female hormones).	By stopping the monthly release of an egg from either ovary, thus preventing fertilization.	Virtually 100% reliable.	Very. Periods are often lighter than normal. Must be prescribed by a doctor. A medical history and examination is necessary and follow-up appointments every six months are required.	Can cause side effects like headaches, acne, weight gain, loss of libido, depression, breast discomfort and others. Also a risk of more serious side effects such as thrombosis and high blood pressure. Very safe for women under 35, but risks increase sharply with age after that. The risks at any age are increased by cigarette-smoking, obesity, diabetes and high blood pressure.	The most suitable method for young women having frequent intercourse. Most GPs prescribe the pill, although they may refuse on medical grounds. It can also be obtained directly from the family planning clinic without seeing a GP.
MINI-PILL (Progestogen only pill)					
A pill taken daily throughout the monthly cycle. It contains a low dose of a synthetic progestogen.	The progestogen inhibits passage of sperm through the cervix and also passage of the egg along the Fallopian tube. Also makes womb lining less receptive to the egg.	Not quite as reliable as the combined pill. Of 100 women on the mini-pill per annum about three become pregnant.	Very. Must be prescribed by a doctor who will take a case history and conduct an examination. Follow-up visits every six months are required.	Even safer than the combined pill because it contains no oestrogen. Minor side effects include irregular breakthrough bleeding. Virtually free of serious side effects.	Suitable for breast-feeding mothers and others for whom an oestrogen-containing pill is unsuitable. Availability – as for the combined pill.
CONDOM (Sheath, French Letter, Male Protective)					
Finger-shaped sheath of thin rubber which is rolled on to the erect penis before intercourse.	Acts as a physical barrier, trapping sperm.	Used carefully, in conjunction with a spermicidal cream, gel or pessary in the vagina, the sheath is quite effective. In 100 couples using this method per annum, four women become pregnant. Without spermicide, about five.	Some couples find it disturbs lovemaking. After ejaculation, the penis must be withdrawn very carefully, whilst still erect, to avoid any of the sperm being spilled. Widely available	None, apart from possible allergy to rubber. Plastic or gut sheaths are available as an alternative.	Useful for 'emergencies' when sex is not anticipated or when other methods are unsuitable. The woman has less direct control when using this method; can also dull the sensation for the male.
CAP (Diaphragm)					
Dome-shaped diaphragm of thin rubber which is inserted into the vagina to cover the cervix shortly before intercourse. Used with spermicidal cream, gel or pessary.	Acts as a physical barrier, preventing sperm in the vagina from reaching the cervix.	Used with spermicidal cream, gel or pessary it is quite effective. Of 100 women using this method per annum, three become pregnant. Very unreliable without spermicide.	Must be the right size. Insertion requires practice. It should not be removed until at least six hours after intercourse. It may detract from the pleasure of some forms of love-play. Must be washed, dried and stored carefully to avoid perishing. Refitting is necessary after childbirth.	None, apart from possible allergy to rubber.	Suitable for occasional or regular sex. Available from chemists on or off prescription. There are several types, of which the larger type, known as the Dutch cap, is most popular.

What it is	How it works	How reliable	How convenient	Hazards	Other comments
IUD (Intra-uterine device, coil, loop)					
Small device, usually plastic, fitted through the cervix, into the womb cavity, by a doctor trained in the technique. It is then left there for two to three years.	Inhibits the action of the womb lining, thus preventing a fertilized egg from implanting in the womb.	Very. Of 100 women using IUDs per annum, about two become pregnant. Occasional failure is sometimes due to expulsion of the IUD by the womb.	Most convenient method, provided the IUD is fitted comfortably. No action need be taken until the next check-up. Fitting sometimes causes initial period-type pains.	Periods may be more painful or heavier. Very slightly increased risk of pelvic infection.	Fitted only by GPs and clinic doctors trained in the technique.
RHYTHM METHOD (Safe period)					
A way of calculating which days in the monthly cycle are safest in terms of avoiding conception, and then confining intercourse to those days.	Conception is only possible in the few days around ovulation (roughly half-way between periods). This 'unsafe' time can be determined by checking dates or detecting the rise in body temperature that accompanies ovulation. This may vary each month. For women whose periods are regular, the unsafe period is between the 10th and 18th days after the period begins.	Of 100 women using the calendar method for a year, about 18 become pregnant. With the temperature method, about 6.	A difficult method for women with irregular periods and a nuisance if temperatures are taken daily. Also restricts the time available for intercourse.	None, apart from the risk of unwanted pregnancy.	Only method acceptable to the Catholic Church.
WITHDRAWAL METHOD (Coitus interruptus)					
Penis is withdrawn from the vagina just before ejaculation.	Sperm do not enter the vagina.	The least reliable of all methods, depending on split-second timing by the man. Using this method, there is a one in four chance of becoming pregnant.	Since climax takes place outside the vagina it is less satisfying for both partners.	None, apart from those resulting from an unwanted pregnancy.	Only to be used as a last resort. Better than no precautions at all.
VASECTOMY (Male sterilization)					
A minor operation on the ducts which carry sperm from the testicles to the prostate gland, where semen is produced. It is performed under local anaesthetic.	Prevents sperm from being added to the semen. Erection, semen production, ejaculation and orgasm are unaffected. Usually irreversible, resulting in permanent sterility.	Virtually 100 per cent reliable.	The operation is simple and safe; minor bruising usually clears within days. However, it may take three months or more before all sperm are cleared from the semen store.	None, apart from some temporary minor post-operative discomfort.	Increasingly popular method for men who have had all the children they want. The operation usually requires a night or two in hospital, although more GPs and family planning clinics are now performing vasectomies. Available free on the NHS, but there may be a long waiting list.
STERILIZATION (Female)					
An operation on the Fallopian tubes, which are either clamped, or tied and cut. Usually performed under general anaesthetic but recent method needs only a local anaesthetic. Usually irreversible, resulting in permanent sterility.	Prevents the eggs being fertilized and entering the womb.	Virtually 100% reliable.	Tubal ligation (tying and cutting the tubes) is usually a major abdominal operation requiring a stay in hospital. Recent methods can be performed on an outpatient basis and only leave small scars.	Usual risks of an abdominal operation.	Suitable for couples who have had all the children they want, but is neither as simple, nor as safe as a vasectomy. Free on NHS but may be long waiting list.

Health on Holiday

Before you go

The golden rule is to plan as far ahead as possible. If you are going anywhere outside Europe, North America, Australia or New Zealand you will almost certainly need a course of vaccinations, some of which may be required by international health regulations. In addition, each country has its own vaccination requirements which may change from year to year, and, depending on the number of vaccinations needed, it may take several weeks to complete the various courses. So as soon as you know where you are going you should ask your travel agent, or airline enquiries desk for details of the vaccinations that are compulsory for the country or countries you will be visiting. Ask, too, about vaccinations that may be advisable but not compulsory; whether or not malaria is present in the countries to be visited; and what other health risks are likely to be encountered. If necessary, more information can be obtained by contacting the relevant Embassy or Consulate.

It's better than being ill on holiday! Your GP can arrange the necessary vaccinations, but remember to allow him enough time.

Compulsory Vaccinations
International health regulations may require valid proof of vaccination against any of three infectious diseases – smallpox, cholera and yellow fever – depending on the countries to be visited. The proof consists of a separate International Certificate of Vaccination against each disease which does not become valid until a specified time after the vaccination. Each traveller, children included, needs a certificate, although there might be important exemptions on medical grounds (for example, some countries will excuse pregnant women, infants and people who have hyper-allergic conditions). In such cases, however, a doctor's letter would have to be produced.

Smallpox According to the World Health Organization (WHO), smallpox has been eradicated worldwide and although there are no medical reasons for it, a few tropical countries still insist on a certificate. Your doctor should be able to perform this vaccination provided he is given sufficient warning. He may charge for either the vaccination or signing the certificate, which becomes valid after eight days (or immediately if it's a *re*-vaccination) and expires after three years. He will also want to know certain details of your medical history to decide whether you may be exempt on grounds of allergy, suppressed immunity, or pregnancy. Infants under one year old are normally exempt.

If a yellow fever vaccination is to accompany the smallpox one, there should be an interval of three weeks to avoid the risk of a reaction.

Cholera This vaccination is compulsory for many countries in the Middle and Far East. Cholera is a potentially fatal diarrhoea widespread throughout the Middle East and North and East Africa. Meticulous attention to the cleanliness of food, drink and hands is the most effective means of protection but travellers to these parts would be well advised to have vaccination even though it may not be a compulsory requirement of the particular country.

It is virtually a necessity for those going on 'trekking' overland holidays which involve a certain amount of living rough. A single injection is usually sufficient and can be given by a GP.

The certificate is valid after six days and expires after six months. Babies under one year old are usually exempt.

Yellow Fever This is a fatal viral infection

spread by mosquitoes. An International Certificate is usually required for travel to or from Central Africa and South America (including the Canal Zone). Yellow fever vaccination has to be done at special centres which will be found in most large towns. Your doctor or travel agent will give you details on request. A single injection is sufficient and the certificate becomes valid ten days later (or at once if it is a revaccination). It expires after ten years. Exemptions are similar to those for smallpox vaccination and it should not be given to infants under nine months old.

Other Important Vaccinations
Although the following vaccinations are not a compulsory public health measure, they are often extremely important for individual and personal protection.

Typhoid and Paratyphoid These serious intestinal infections are widespread throughout the world outside Northern Europe, Canada, USA, Australia or New Zealand. They are particularly common around the Mediterranean, North Africa, the Middle East and India. Not only are they a major health hazard to campers and overlanders in these areas, but also to package tour holidaymakers staying in newly built resorts which have dubious sewage systems.

Typhoid and paratyphoid are usually combined in a single vaccine called TAB (sometimes also including tetanus protection – TABT). The full course, which your doctor should be able to arrange, consists of two injections, given 4 to 6 weeks apart (or, if you are in a great hurry, not less than ten days) with a booster 6 to 12 months later. Protection lasts about three years.

Tetanus (Lockjaw) This is a usually fatal infection causing violent spasms. It is contracted when dirt is allowed to penetrate, and thus contaminate, deep cuts and grazes. Although tetanus can be contracted in the UK, it is much commoner in warm climates. Once again, campers and overlanders are at particular risk as too are children, who, in their holiday enthusiasm are that much more likely to trip and cut themselves.

If a tetanus injection has been given in the past (usually as part of the triple vaccine in infancy), a single booster dose will suffice. Protection lasts at least ten years.

Polio This is still a major health hazard in warm climates or where sanitation is dubious. If you are travelling outside Northern Europe, Canada, USA, Australia or New Zealand, you would be well advised to have this vaccination (which is usually given on a sugar lump, *not* by injection). If a smallpox or yellow fever vaccination is required as well, allow a space of three weeks to avoid reactions. Boosters are necessary about every five years.

Plague, Typhus and Infective Hepatitis
Vaccination against these diseases are really only necessary for travellers to Indo-China, the Indian subcontinent and Central Africa, especially those who are going overland.

Protection against Malaria Malaria is a potentially fatal fever caught by being bitten by an infected mosquito. Every year, more and more travellers get home to this country and suddenly succumb to an attack of malaria. The disease is commonplace throughout the tropics and subtropics, including North Africa and the Middle East. Your travel agent will tell you whether malaria is present in the places you are visiting, or if there is any doubt, consult the relevant Embassy or Consulate.

It is vital to protect yourself against malaria by taking regular anti-malarial tablets (there is no vaccination available). You should start taking the pills about a week before you arrive in a malarious area; then take them for the whole time you stay there and for 28 days afterwards. It is most important to follow this procedure even if only passing through a malaria infected country. The disease can be contracted from one bite.

Anti-malarial tablets can be bought cheaply and without prescription from chemists. Some airlines will provide them on the plane.

Other Precautions
Medical treatment may be hard to come by (or very expensive) in foreign countries, so it is worth considering a few other sensible precautions before holidaying abroad. It is wise, for example, to take along a few useful medications. Such simple items as a packet of soluble aspirin or paracetamol tablets, anti-diarrhoea tablets, travel sickness pills, insect repellent cream, sunscreen lotion, antiseptic cream and a few adhesive dressings could help to save a lot of trouble and misery. Sufferers from any chronic disease or disability should always consult their doctor before embarking on a journey by air or sea, especially if the trip is for more than a week or so. It may be a good idea to take a few written details of the condition, including allergies and any medication being taken.

It is worthwhile to take out insurance against accidental injury and medical expenses whilst abroad.

On the Way

By air

Most holiday flights are fairly short, but even so some people will still experience 'in flight' health problems.

Apart from the sheer fear of flying, the commonest problem is acute ear discomfort caused by the reduced cabin pressure. This is always worse if you have a cold or catarrh which blocks the tubes connecting nasal passages to the ears. Decongestant nosedrops or inhaler may help, or try yawning, or pinching your nose and swallowing.

Motion sickness is another problem although it is fairly unusual in these days of smooth jet travel. It helps a little to avoid alcohol and fatty foods before and during the flight, and to sit over the wings of the plane. Undoubtedly the most effective way of preventing motion sickness is to take an anti-sickness pill about an hour before the flight. Long flights can cause considerable discomfort simply because of having to sit in a seat for hours on end. It helps if you stretch your legs by walking in the aisles when the opportunity presents itself.

Another problem occurs with long flights in an east/west or west/east direction. Widely known as 'jet lag', it is the disturbance of the traveller's normal daily body rhythms caused by flying rapidly between time zones. Westward flights lengthen the 'day', while eastward flights shorten it. Either way it upsets the traveller's pattern of eating, sleeping and waking and the overall effect is to induce fatigue, irritability, indecisiveness and disturbed sleep and bowel habits. Such symptoms can continue for three to four days afterwards. To minimize jet lag, try to arrive at your destination as near as possible to your normal bedtime and go straight to bed.

By sea

The main problem when travelling by sea is motion sickness (sea-sickness), which, in fact, is often brought on by anxiety about the *possibility* of feeling sick. It helps to avoid alcohol and too much fatty food. Some people find that lying down amidships with their eyes closed seems to ward off sickness, while others prefer to walk about on the open deck and 'ride' the seas. The most effective way of preventing sea sickness is to take an anti-sickness pill about an hour before leaving harbour and another every few hours.

By land

Car sickness can be a problem. It may be averted by looking out of the front or back window rather than the sides, letting in plenty of fresh air whilst driving along and stopping frequently to get out and stretch your legs. Again, anti-sickness pills are usually effective.

While you are away

The most likely health hazards faced by holidaymakers in hot sunny climes are some form of gastric or intestinal infection or problems with the heat, such as heat exhaustion or sunburn. Traveller's diarrhoea is one of the commonest afflictions that beset holidaymakers, and many an expensive fortnight on the sun-drenched Mediterranean has been swamped by waves of nausea, griping abdominal pains and unending diarrhoea. Like other gastro-intestinal infections such as typhoid, paratyphoid and cholera, it is caused by poor standards of hygiene and sanitation contaminating the traveller's food and drink.

If you are camping or self-catering you must take extra care to avoid tummy upsets. Cook your food thoroughly and wash salads and fruit carefully.

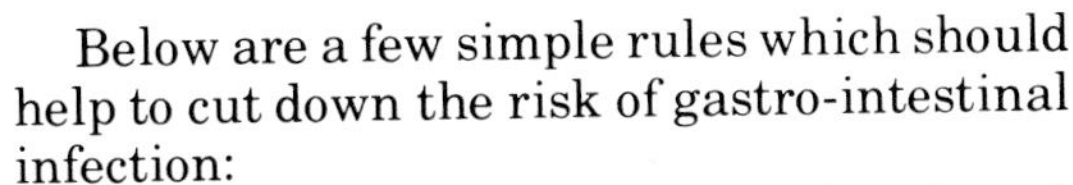

Below are a few simple rules which should help to cut down the risk of gastro-intestinal infection:

1. Beware the local water, even in a brand new hotel. Ideally you should always boil it, or sterilize it with chlorine tablets before drinking it, or brushing your teeth with it. This is essential for overland travellers in North Africa, the Middle East and the Indian subcontinent.
2. Whenever possible, drink only well-known brands of bottled minerals. Wipe the tops of bottles well – the ice in the icebox may be contaminated.
3. Boil all milk and do not eat local ices. Again, stick to well-known brands.
4. Keep all food away from flies – they are almost certainly heavily contaminated.
5. Eat only recently cooked food, never re-heated food or food left uncovered.
6. Peel all uncooked fruit. Beware salads which may have been washed in contaminated water.
7. Choose your restaurants very carefully.
8. Be very wary about eating shellfish.

Heat Problems

These are caused either by excessive sweating or by disturbance to the body's temperature regulating system as a result of the sudden change in climate. It can take several days to acclimatize and if, before then, you rush about and sweat considerably, or drink alcohol whilst lying in the sun, there is a great risk of heat exhaustion and the much more dangerous heatstroke.

Heat Exhaustion is caused by excessive sweating, leading to loss of fluid and salt from the body. This gives rise to headache, queasiness, a shivery feeling and lethargy. Treatment is to rest in the cool shade and drink plenty of fruit juice containing a little salt – one teaspoon per litre (2 pints).

Heat Stroke is caused by a sudden breakdown in the temperature regulating system. The victim feels feverish and may have a dizzy headache. He feels hot and dry to the touch and his temperature rapidly soars upwards as he loses consciousness. This is a medical emergency and the vital course of action is to cool down the victim as rapidly as possible. Cover him with a soaking wet sheet and keep it cool by vigorous fanning.

How to Avoid Heat Problems

Drink plenty of fluids, but avoid alcohol during the day. Avoid too much physical exertion in the first few days of your holiday and wear loose clothing of cotton or natural fibres. Put extra salt on food.

Sunburn This is another classic way of ruining a holiday. Pale-skinned people and children are especially susceptible and should not spend more than 15 to 20 minutes exposed to the sun for the first day or two. There is a wide range of skin preparations for protection against sunburn and these are discussed more fully on page 14.

Mosquitoes

Apart from causing considerable discomfort with their bites, these insects can transmit malaria and yellow fever in those parts of the world where these diseases are prevalent (see page 71). Avoid them by:

1. Staying indoors at dusk, dawn and at night, if possible. Keep your skin well covered after dark.
2. Insist on mosquito-proof mesh over the windows and netting over the bed.
3. Cover exposed skin with insect repellent and spray the room with aerosol insecticide.
4. Take anti-malarial tablets regularly before, throughout and after your stay.

Home again

Do not let the relief of being home safe and well allow you to forget to continue with the anti-malarial tablets. Also, any sudden minor fever or diarrhoea symptoms that may occur in any member of the family should be reported to your doctor without delay.

Happy Ever After

A new start

Retirement obviously involves fundamental readjustments to the way you live your life. After a lifetime of working for others, there is suddenly time for yourself. Furthermore you must cope with a substantial cut in income, the missing of workmates and possibly a fall in self esteem. Clearly the people who adjust most easily to retirement will be those who have prepared themselves for it.

Money matters

Your financial affairs will certainly require some pre-planning. Sorting out pension rights and benefits can be a complicated business, and help is available from local Social Security Offices. Private pension schemes may have to be discussed with your firm's finance officer or your bank manager before retirement. Your bank manager or your local Citizens' Advice Bureau can advise you on savings, investment and questions related to your tax position. Such matters are important in planning a retirement budget and helping to decide whether it is wise to take another full-time or part-time paid job.

To move or not to move

Another major consideration is whether or not to move house. Many newly retired people feel they would like to move to somewhere they have always wanted to live: perhaps near the sea, or near some member of their family. Think carefully before making such a move, though. Moving to a new area will mean leaving old friends and neighbours and it may not be easy to settle into a relatively unfamiliar environment.

Consider, too, the practicalities of daily life in the new area. Such mundane aspects as the availability of public transport assume greater importance as you get older. Is the new area easily accessible to friends and relatives, making it possible for them to visit regularly? Are the local health facilities (health centre, hospital) reasonably close?

Time to consider

The other major aspect of retirement is what to do with all your newly acquired time. It brings so many new opportunities for leisure activities, study, voluntary work, part-time or even full-time employment, that it can be extremely difficult to make a decision.

This may be easier if you ask yourself a few basic questions: do you need to keep working for the extra money it brings in or because you would be discontented without some sort of job? Do you have skills that could earn you money or be used to help other people? Are there any particular people to whom you would like to devote more time? Which interests or activities would you like to take up now that you have the time?

Despite high unemployment there are many job opportunities (mostly part-time) suitable for retired people. If this is what you want to do ask among friends and colleagues, perhaps before you retire. Alternatively, enquire at your local Job Centre or employment agencies, or study advertisements in the local paper and newsagents' boards. Your local pensioners' action group or Citizens' Advice Bureau may also be able to advise you.

If you are happy to work unpaid there are scores of opportunities to help with local voluntary activities. Once again your Citizens' Advice Bureau will be able to advise. Another possibility is to go back to school – this time for enjoyment! A comprehensive range of studies and courses is available; such as correspondence courses, adult education classes, courses at residential colleges, and even the Open University. The district library will give you information on adult education opportunities, or you can contact your local education authority.

Making the most of your health

With perhaps a decade or two ahead, it's vital for those of retirement age to retain as much of their good health as possible. Keeping in shape is very important if one is to get the most out of retirement.

Now that you are an older person, some of the health principles discussed previously will assume greater importance for you. As the years go by, one of the body's most fundamental processes, namely the automatic repair and replacement of tissues, slows down and becomes erratic. This causes the characteristic changes of ageing and if left entirely to its own devices, the body would soon falter into a state of ill-health and dependence on the help of others. Fortunately, an elderly person's body is quite capable of tissue repair and replacement, providing this process is stimulated by making the right effort.

Exercise

Regular attention to exercise is perhaps the best way to stimulate body maintenance. 'Use it or lose it' is the rule. All the general principles of exercise expounded in the chapter on Fitness (page 48) apply to all age groups, but for people of retirement age the emphasis is a little different. For instance, whilst stamina (see page 51) is still important, it is perhaps less so than suppleness, because joints tend to stiffen with disuse much more quickly as they get older. This can soon hamper mobility and agility. There are three basic rules to keeping (or getting) fit in retirement:

1. Any exercise is better than none at all.
2. It's never too late to start.
3. Exercise should be part of an *everyday* activity plan.

Keeping fit involves taking various forms of exercise each day; including some stretching and bending – to maintain the mobility of spine and joints; some stamina exercises, such as walking, swimming, or cycling – to build up the reserves of the cardiovascular system (heart, blood vessels, lungs) so that circulation improves and you do not get breathless so easily; and some strength exercises – to improve muscle function and protect bones and joints from sudden strain and minor injury.

People who are fairly active may find that many of these movements are contained in their usual activities, such as gardening, handiwork, housework or playing golf. However it is important to make sure some aspects of exercise are not neglected and to this end, it may help to have a routine for keeping yourself in shape.

The food you eat

A balanced diet is essential for good health at any age but, in particular, the elderly should pay particular attention to three main aspects: vitamins, calories and fibre.

Vitamins

Older people can easily lose interest in food, for all sorts of reasons, and can quite quickly become vitamin deficient. If you cannot shop or cook for yourself, get a relative, neighbour or the local social services department to help you. It is very important to have at least one proper meal a day. Even then it is possible to go short of some vitamins, notably those listed below (with the main foods in which they are found). Make sure, therefore, your diet contains a good selection of these foods.

Vitamin C – fresh citrus fruits, leafy vegetables, salads, potatoes in their jackets, or a daily dose of blackcurrant or rose-hip syrup. (Do not overcook vegetables; heat destroys vitamin C.)

B vitamins – liver (or liver pâté), kidneys, dairy products, leafy vegetables, legumes, cereals and wholemeal bread.

Vitamin D – margarine, fatty fish (mackerel, herring, sardines), eggs and milk. Try to get plenty of sun (which makes vitamin D in the skin).

Calories

You should weigh no more in retirement than in your twenties (see weight chart page 25), but it is likely that you will need fewer calories per day to sustain this weight. Excess weight puts a heavy load on your back, joints and feet, making arthritis and foot trouble that much worse or that much more likely. Turn to page 28 for advice on how to lose weight.

Fibre

Whilst plenty of dietary fibre is an important part of a balanced diet all through life, it is particularly so as old age approaches. Diverticular disease is the presence of small blown-out pockets in the large intestine and it affects one in three people over the age of 60. It is caused by high pressures in the intestine brought about by slow movement of its contents and by constipation. The best way to reduce the risk of developing diverticular disease and its consequences is to eat plenty of food containing dietary fibre, such as wholemeal bread, wholewheat cereals, wheatbran, leafy vegetables and fresh fruit. (See page 26 for further details.)

Older people need more fibre, fewer calories and plenty of vitamins.

Some special problems

Failing vision

From teenage onwards, the lenses of the eyes gradually harden and lose their elasticity so that it becomes difficult to focus on close objects (**presbyopia**). Most people over about 45 years old can only read small print at arm's length and have to wear convex glasses for reading or sewing. 'Floaters' – specks apparently floating in front of the eyes – are common in older people. Although they are often annoying, they only rarely interfere with vision and do not signify the onset of blindness.

However, partial blindness is a problem that besets a sizeable minority of elderly people. The commonest cause is a blurring of vision due to degenerative processes affecting the blood vessels that supply the retina at the back of the eye. Another common cause is cataract, in which the lens becomes more and more opaque, making vision cloudy and giving bright lights a halo effect. These conditions can usually be treated successfully if they are discovered soon enough. Elderly people should have their eyes tested *at least* every two years, and more frequently if their sight is worsening rapidly. Anyone suffering a *sudden* blurring of vision should be taken to a hospital emergency department or a local eye hospital at once.

Hearing difficulties

Some loss of hearing is a part of normal ageing and by the age of about 60, higher frequencies – such as the phone or doorbell ringing – may be quite difficult to hear.

Most elderly people resign themselves to being 'a little hard of hearing' and fail to seek help. This is foolish because the trouble may be something as simple and treatable as wax in the ear (see page 16). With more permanent conditions, hearing can nearly always be greatly improved with a hearing aid. As soon as you think your hearing is deteriorating, see your doctor.

If you are with someone who is hard of hearing, do not mumble or shout. Instead enunciate slowly and clearly at normal volume and stand where your lips can be clearly seen.

Memory

Elderly people are often accused of being absent-minded, and they frequently use muddle-headedness or poor memory as an excuse for not thinking or doing anything. In fact, the reverse is usually the case. Memory and clear thinking are skills that can be acquired by dint of will-power and determination and this applies to all ages, including the elderly. Keeping the mind sharp means keeping it busy.

Foot problems

It has been calculated that in the course of a lifetime the average person walks approximately 120,000 km (75,000 miles). It is hardly surprising therefore that the feet begin to show a few signs of wear and tear at retirement age.

Arches can flatten, soles spread and toes become crooked and splayed. Tendons can stretch, ligaments loosen, corns ripen and bunions bulge. Circulation in legs and feet can get sluggish; the skin becoming cold, thin and quick to fester, with fungus thriving between toes and invading horny toenails. Of course the feet of many elderly people are not necessarily as troubled as this, but in fact, even one or two of these problems can be enough to restrict mobility severely.

Fortunately all the problems mentioned above can be greatly helped by seeking expert advice and treatment. Generally, the doctor should be consulted first and he can arrange for chiropody or orthopaedic treatment where necessary.

There is a lot one can do personally to improve or ward off such conditions. Keep feet free of skin (and nail) trouble by following the advice on page 12. Wear well-fitting shoes at all times (slippers do *not* provide enough support and can cause aching arches). Make sure shoes are comfortable before buying them – it should not be necessary to 'break them in'.

If your feet are so out of shape that no ordinary shoes will fit, your doctor can arrange for suitable orthopaedic footwear to be made. Finally, do not try to cut corns, nor use so-called corn cures, nor struggle to cut toenails that are hard to reach. Instead, see a chiropodist.

Hypothermia

Because the circulation in the skin becomes rather sluggish most elderly people tend to feel the cold more acutely. By wearing warm clothes – socks and stocking in particular – and staying in warm surroundings, this is generally not too much of a problem. In such circumstances, body temperatures will remain normal at about 37°C (98·4°F).

However, one in ten people over the age of 65 has a body temperature at least 1½°C (3°F) below normal. This is either because the surroundings are so cold that they simply cannot keep warm or because the body's temperature control system is not functioning properly, even in relatively warm surroundings. In either case there is a risk of slipping into

Family togetherness. Do not forget to keep grandparents in the picture.

hypothermia (body temperature of below 35°C (95°F). This happens over a period of hours or days, until below a temperature of 32·5°C (90°F), the mind becomes sluggish and movements laboured. The person becomes confused, drowsy and finally loses consciousness.

The risk of hypothermia can be greatly reduced by a few simple precautions. Try to keep at least one room really warm and if possible use that room for sleeping. Make sure that draughts under doors, around windows and between floorboards are sealed, and that curtains are suitably lined. Wear warm clothes (wool is best and several layers are better than one thick layer). Gloves and socks help, and so does a hat – even indoors, because about one-fifth of body heat may be lost from a bare head. Put plenty of blankets – or better still, a duvet – on the bed, use a hot water bottle or electric blanket and always put on a dressing gown and socks – if you get up at night. During the day, move about as much as possible and eat and drink hot food rather than cold.

Ask the local Social Services department (at the Town Hall) for advice on home heating allowances and other grants.

Helping Hands

Fortunately the great majority of our elderly people are loved and well cared for by relatives and friends. Of course, nobody wants to be a nuisance to others and elderly people quite rightly like to be as independent as possible. This can sometimes cause problems – friends and relatives might be over-zealous, while an old person's self-respect might prevent him or her from summoning help when it is needed. As in so many things, it is a question of striking the right balance.

Those old people who are in particular need of help include those who are housebound, frail and lonely and have no caring relatives, friends or neighbours. Try to make sure they are not neglected.

There are so many different ways to be helpful to someone who is old. It may be no more than dropping in for a chat or offering to do some shopping. It may be cooking a meal, or fetching in the coal, or taking them to the doctor, or contacting a community care service on their behalf.

There is a large number of official and voluntary organizations involved in providing help for old people at home – anything from mobility allowances, home helps or 'meals-on-wheels' (provided by the local social services department) to investment counsellors, handymen and 'good companions' (from local voluntary groups). The aim is always to help old people to live independently in the community.

Index

Acknowledgements

The author would like to thank the HEALTH EDUCATION COUNCIL for its invaluable help as a source of information and guidance in the preparation of this book.

The publishers would like to thank the following for their kind permission to reproduce the photographs in this book: Special Photography: **Sandra Lousada** 1, 2–3, 4–5, 6–7, 10–11, 12–13, 14, 23, 46–47, 48–49, 58–59, 63, 64–65, 70–71, 74–75, 78–79; **Chris Harvey** 8–9, 19, 42–43, 44, 45, 52, 54, 55, 56, 57; **Spike Powell** 17, 18, 20–21, 40–41, 53, 60–61; **Peter Rauter** 26, 28–29, 36–37, 38, 76–77; **Mike Bale** 30–31; **Zefa Picture Library** (Erwin Christian) 68–69, (H. Helmlinger) 72–73 above, (R. H. Jarosch) 72–73 below.

Cover photography: **Chris Harvey**

The publishers would also like to thank the following for kindly lending their products for the photographs: **Marks and Spencer Ltd:** range of children's clothes, red kitchenware, towels and toiletries, sportswear and ladies' outfits; **Animus:** Alresford teddy bear; **Laura Ashley:** camisole, petticoat, dressing-gown and nightdress; **Detail:** necklace and earrings; **Mothercare:** baby's high chair; **Kite Store:** Malay kite; **E. Chamberlaine:** Raleigh traveller.

Presented to
Cameron Watson
Urray Free Church
Sunday school
June '04
CHILDREN'S MINISTRY
CLC BOOKSHOPS

STORIES JESUS TOLD

Illustrated by Chris Rothero

It's fun to Read Along

Here's what you do –

These pictures are some of the characters and things the story tells about. Let the child to whom you are reading SEE and SAY them.

Then, as you read the story text and come to a picture instead of a word, pause and point to the picture for your listener to SEE and SAY.

You'll be amazed at how quickly children catch on and enjoy participating in the story telling.

Sower

Soldiers

Shepherd

Mother

Traveller

Stable Boy

Bandits

Wife

Good Samaritan

Inn

Inn Keeper

Gold

ISBN 1-84135-035-4

First published 1992
This edition first published 2000

Reprinted 2002

Published by Award Publications Limited,
1st Floor, 27 Longford Street, London NW1 3DZ

Printed in Malaysia

The Sower and his Seed

Early one morning a  filled his  with  and went into his field to sow them.

Some  fell on the road and the  flew down from the  and ate them.

Some  landed in a thorn 

and the long sharp thorns choked the

tiny and they died.

But the  went on sowing his

 until his  was empty,

and all the rest of his  fell on

ground that was good.

These tiny  grew and grew into

a field of lovely golden corn.

The Lost Sheep

A  cares for every one of his

 . There was once a good 

who was ready to fight a 

or a  for his .

One night this good  counted

his  as usual only to find there

was one missing. One of his 

was lost.

The  were bright in the night

sky as the  began his search for the lost  . He heard a

 howl and he was afraid. After

a long search he found his lost 

and carried it home.

The  didn’t mind being so

tired. He was just happy that his lost

 was safe.

The Good Samaritan

One day a weary  was riding along a lonely road when suddenly, fierce  sprang at him from the  .

The  dragged him from his  and took everything he had, even some of his  .

The  lay half-dead at the road side with the hot  beating down on him.

Soon along that narrow road people

came – a  on a fine  ,

another on a  . Both men

looked the other way when they saw

the poor wounded  and

hurried on.

Then round the bend came another

man on a  . This was the  .

He stopped and went to help the dying  . He gave him water to drink and bound up his wounds before lifting him on to his  and taking him to the nearest  .

"Take care of this poor  ," said the  to the  . "Here are some silver  . If you spend more I will repay you on my return ...!"

"I will indeed," said the  , wishing that all men had kind hearts like the  .

The King and the Cruel Servant

There was once a powerful 
who lived in a fine  . One day
the  discovered that his
trusted  had cheated him out
of a huge amount of  .
"You must pay back what you owe!"
cried the angry  , "or go to

prison."

"I cannot!" wailed the ,

falling on his knees. "I have a 

and two  ..."

The  was moved to pity as the

 begged for forgiveness. "I

forgive you," he said at last. "And

you need not pay back the  ."

In high spirits the  left the  .

But at the  who should he meet

but the young  !

The  was leading a  .

"Stop!" shouted the  . "You owe me money!"

"I cannot pay you," said the 

tearfully. "Forgive me! I have an old

 to look after ..."

"I won't forgive you!" cried the cruel

 . "Never!"

And he told the  to put the

 in prison.

The next day the  sent for the cruel  .

"I showed you mercy," he said in a stern voice. "I forgave you. But you, in your turn, did not forgive that poor  ." And the  ordered his  to throw the cruel  into one of the deepest dungeons in his  .